The
CENTRAL
Significance
of
CULTURE

by
FRANCIS NIGEL LEE

ISBN 0-9773442-0-7

Publisher:
Reformation Media and Press
13950 - 122nd St.
Fellsmere, Florida 32948-6411 U.S.A.
rcmc@direcway.com

2005
Reformation Media and Press

Robert M. Metcalf, Jr.
Christian businessman
Christian gentleman
Christian Christian

The
CENTRAL
Significance
of
CULTURE

The contents of this book are lectures given in the summer of 1974 at the Summer Institute of the Christian Studies Center, P.O. Box 17122, Memphis, TN 38117.

Cover graphic: Larno Meyer and Francis Nigel Lee

Culture and Calvary's cross and Christ's Kingship (1 Cor. 15:1-4, 58) all root in the infallible Word of God (2 Tim. 3:16-17).

Christ reigns over all of life (Rom. 11:36) —

over and through the scales, in *physics* (Is. 40:12);
over and through sportsmen, in *athletics* (1 Cor. 9:24);
over and through microscopes, in *biology* (Ps. 104:25);
over and through swords, in *warfare* (Ps. 144:1);
over and through coins, in *commerce* (Matt. 20:28);
over and through notes, in *music* (Ps. 150:3);
over and through judges, in *politics* (Ex. 22:9);
over and through blueprints, in *architecture* (Gen. 4:17);
over and through brushes, in *aesthetics* (Ps. 68:13);
over and through cogwheels, in *industry* (Gen. 4:22);
over and through schools, in *education* (Acts 19:9).

All things were created by Him and for Him (Col. 1:16), and He reconciled *all* things through the blood of His cross (Col. 1:20).

TABLE OF CONTENTS

CHRISTIANITY AND THE HISTORY OF CULTURE

Free Translations from Rev. Prof. Dr. Klaas Schilder

"Paradise was the *beginning*. And in that *beginning*, everything was already there in principle that had to be there in potential, in order for it to develop into a *consummated* world. But a historical *process* of many centuries is needed for it to come to its full-grown state. . . .

"Sin disturbed things: man fell away from God. Everything started coming apart. Man's life was broken. . . . But Christ conquers the world for His God! He unites the beginnings of the world with its final end, its earliest history with its ultimate history, its alpha with its omega, the abc of God's legislative speech in the *beginning* to the composition of the fugue of the faithful culture of the last days, ripe in all its points and counterpoints. . . . For the *abc* of God's laws dominates all spheres of life. And in all this, Christ consummates everything in the world. . . . He went back to the beginning of God's creation; there from the tables of the law He read out the rules for work laid down at the beginning by God for the 'man-of-God' who was God's creature *in* and *with* the world. And *this* is the pure rule for labor which He read out from the table of the law: that every laborer God created, should, in the history of the created world, so use all the 'talents' issued by God to His workmen in the *morning* of creation, that, by making them productive, *everything inherent in the world would finally be extracted from it.* All the talents which the Lord of the servants gave to the servants, were finally to have achieved just as much at dusk, as they were distributed at dawn to do. . . .

"It was to make this *service* of God again possible for man, to give God His world and His workmen back again, that Christ came.

. . . With His *blood* He purchases a Church, as His heir to eternal life. But inasmuch as eternal life must commence *here and now,* yes, *here,* in this *world of culture* . . . , through His Holy Spirit He *prepares* His blood-bought laborers for the service of God. He gives back to the *new humanity*—which *was* the old!—the rich powers of His poured-out Spirit: the powers of sanctification, of ecclesiastical conquest, of world cultivation, of cultural activity. . . . He again makes 'men of God.' Amid a crooked and perverse generation, He again erects specimens of the *pure* human race. They are not yet perfect, but in principle they *do* exist. They exist from the very moment Adam bowed in faith under the first Gospel promise, and they are coming, and increasing, and becoming the great multitude which no man can number, the multitude of those sanctified by God in Christ. Their army is increasing, and shall be completely numbered by the last day."

—*Jezus Christus en het cultuurleven,* pp. 250-257.

"Kings and nations—both have sought their glory and honor. And in Babylon's shining cultural life they gathered for themselves treasures, brought their luxuries together, and put everything in order with the thoroughness of hands experienced in arranging wealth and with the patience of one who thinks he controls time (Rev. 18: 15, 23).

"Shall culture have blossomed in vain? Must all that wealth disappear without a trace? Is God's day of judgment a furious iconoclasm, a blind and total and unsparing destruction of everything that is?

"Scripture knows nothing of this! Babylon has not lived in vain, and neither has she garnered and guarded her riches in vain. . . . That which is sinful in Babylon's culture is to be burned away. But that which is *cultural* in Babylon's sin—*that* God will not reject. . . . When God's New Jerusalem—His city of peace—comes down from God out of heaven, culture, then divested of its sinful stains, shall surrender its fruits to God's Kingdom. The glory and the honor, not only of the kings, but also of the nations—yet not only of the masses, but also of that in which the individual brilliance of the style-formers and the pace-setters is to be seen—will all be brought into God's new paradise of the future (Rev. 21:24-26). . . .

"Thus it is precisely the Calvinistic life and world view which accepts a life's task which arouses the highest tension of the soul in the knowledge that there is a vocation in respect of the entire cosmos which rests on that man who hears creation sigh for *his* own sake, and who hears God's voice calling him to enter into the sabbath of God: for God's sabbath arrives when the cosmos is renewed and the universe is regenerated. The psalm which commences with the confession that our building up of the house of the universe is in vain unless God Himself is put first in that construction, ends with the heroic image of the man with a full quiver who puts the full armor of God onto his sons to undertake the conquest of the world for his and their God." (Ps. 127; cf. Gen. 1:26-28; I Cor. 3:9, and Heb. 4:4-11.)

— *De Openbaring van Johannes en het Sociale Leven,* pp. 207-9, 238-9.

FOREWORD

The word *culture* is very familiar to the South African ear. However, whether we always understand the full meaning and scope of culture is another matter. And it is clear that we do not always take account of the possibility—and reality—of bad culture, the result of the fall, and of the necessity to proclaim Christ's kingship over the entire cultural terrain.

This cultural inspiration or efflux, although sometimes very perverted, is also manifested among non-Christian nations, and may frequently be enjoyed by Christians. It is the fruit of God's common grace, whereby He maintains His work in man; but that does not detract from the fact that it is only by way of obedience to Christ that bad culture or man-centered culture can be transformed into culture which glorifies God.

Dr. Nigel Lee has devoted serious study to this matter and constantly asks the reader: What saith the Scripture? This study is worthy of attentive investigation. It offers a wide outlook on the cultural command and the work of man in all areas of life as a commission of God, Who is also the Lord of culture. The theocentric approach is basic to the writer's approach, even for culture too, namely, "Of Him and through Him and to Him are all things: to Whom be glory for ever" (Rom. 11:36).

Dr. A. P. Treurnicht, M.P.
Member of Parliament, S.A. Congress
Cape Town, Republic of South Africa

INTRODUCTION

Professor C. N. Venter, Ph.D.
Chairman, Department of Cultural Science
University of Potchefstroom for Christian Higher Education
South Africa

It was indeed a happy day for me when Prof. S. C. W. Duvenage, director of the Institute for the Promotion of Calvinism and chairman of the Department of Biblical Science at the University of Potchefstroom for Christian Higher Education, put this book into my hands.

I will have to bridle my enthusiasm for the sake of appropriate self-control lest I write in the superlative degree about this book.

Dr. Nigel Lee is a many-sided and very learned man with rows of titles behind his name — and he is still busy acquiring more. So far he has received most of his degrees *cum laude.* In addition to being a philosopher, a jurist, etc., etc., he is also a theologian and an ordained minister of the Dutch Reformed Church in South Africa. He was chairman of the Department of Philosophy and Religion at Shelton College in Cape May, New Jersey, U.S.A., when this book was first written.

Dr. Lee was born in 1934 — thus he is still relatively young, and we can therefore still expect much of this thorough Calvinist-without-apology, this tried-and-tested Reformed theologian and great and comprehensive scholar—that is to say, if this book is an accurate reflection of the kind of work which can constantly be expected of him in the future. . . . It was a pleasure to read a rare exposition of a Calvinistic view of culture—and all of it doctrinally well supported and documented with scriptural references.

The Triune God is the actual and great Creator and Maintainer and Consummator of culture, believes Dr. Lee. On the basis of the covenant of works, Adam, and in him mankind, is obliged to complete the cultural task ("Be fruitful and multiply and replenish the earth, subdue it and have dominion . . . to dress it and keep it"—Gen. 1:28; 2:15).

Sin occurs, and Christ (the incarnate Word) acts immediately as Mediator to keep the covenant of works and to save the entire creation (with the exception of the unbelievers) by so having dominion over it that He recreates it as Dominator (that is to say, as The Cultivator *par excellence*)—and He rules with man as His co-worker, until culture (the work of God's hands) reaches its consummation in the New Jerusalem.

Even man's dispersion and population of the earth is directly caused by God. The elect of every nation bring into the New Jerusalem even the (purified) culture of the unbelievers from each distinct nation, in addition to their own culture; for it is God's culture, His own handwork, and thus His honor and glory, which is brought into the New Jerusalem by the kings and the nations (Rev. 21:24-26). Even the South African culture and folklore will be glorified and brought into the New Jerusalem—even in the literally "material" sense. And the latter point of view concerning the literally "material" nature of the New Jerusalem is scientifically and well documented.

The whole work breathes the Spirit of a strongly Reformed theological atmosphere with a reasonably strict "Kuyperian approach." For the rest, the book will have to be left to the critical judgment of Reformed exegetes in the course of time. I believe Dr. Lee will even welcome that.

I

THE ROOTS OF CULTURE

What *is* Culture? Where did it initially come from, and how did it originally *start*?

According to the famous communist Vladimir Lenin, culture first started when "a herd of apes grasped sticks"[1] and thereby evolved into human beings.

Lenin's predecessor, Karl Marx's famous colleague Frederick Engels, however, gives us a rather more detailed account. According to Engels, in his book *The Part Played by Labor in the Transition from Ape to Man,*[2] after man left the trees and quit walking on all-fours on the ground, he began to use his hands "to perform hundreds of operations that no monkey's hand can imitate.[3] For "no simian [or ape-like] hand ever fashioned even the crudest of stone knives,"[3] as the first *men* did. And this, believes Engels, represents the origin of culture, especially when man's manual 'cult-ivation' of "fire separated him forever from the animal world."[4] And further, he added, labor and speech were the two most essential stimuli under the influence of which the brain of the ape gradually changed into that of man.[5]

Similarly, Karl Marx himself fully agrees with Benjamin Franklin's

1. Lenin, *The State and Revolution,* as quoted in Wetter, *Philosophie und Naturwissenschaft in der Sowjetunion* (Hamburg, Germany: Rowohlt, 1958), p. 97.
2. Cf. in Marx and Engels, *Selected Works* (Moscow, Soviet Union: Foreign Languages Publishing House, 1951), vol. II.
3. Engels, *The Part Played by Labor in the Transition from Ape to Man,* in Marx and Engels, *op. cit.,* II, 75.
4. Engels, *Anti-Dühring* (London: Lawrence and Wishart, 1934), p. 129.
5. Engels, *The Part Played by Labor . . . ,* p. 77.

definition of "man as a 'tool-making animal.' "[6] For although spiders make webs and bees make honeycombs (yet never houses!), inasmuch as nature itself "constructs no machines, no locomotives, railways, electric telegraphs, self-acting mules, etc.," these latter, writes Marx, are all "products of *human* industry, natural material transformed into instruments for the *human domination of nature.*"[7] As man the laborer works, Marx explains further, even "nature becomes one of the organs of his activity, one that he *annexes* to himself. . . . As the earth is his original larder, so too is it his original tool house."[8]

Essentially similar are the views of many modern evolutionists in the free world too, such as those of Ritchie Calder, professor of international relations at Edinburgh University in Scotland. While still facetiously presupposing God's seven days' formation of the world, in his book, *After the Seventh Day—the World [that] Man Created,*[9] Calder traces the progress of culture and technology from what he believes to be its origins. Leaning heavily on his friend the Fabian socialist H. G. Wells,[10] Calder, like Franklin, Boswell, and Marx, is happy to categorize "Man [with a capital 'M'!] as a tool-making animal."[11] And he further avers that this human cultural ability, remotely rooted in the digital dexterity of prosimians such as the supposedly 50-million-year-old assumed ancestors of the tree shrews and the lemurs and the tarsiers, in time evolved into various now-extinct anthropoids such as Proconsul and hominids such as the Australopithecines. These, he tells us, were "the creatures who were either our grand-to-the-nth-fathers or our great-to-the-nth-uncles,"[12] until, as Engels too avers,[4] we finally arrive at their more recent and more

---

6. Marx, *Capital* (London: Geo. Allen & Unwin, 1938), I, 152. Cf. too Kraan, *Een Christelijke Confrontatie met Marx, Lenin, en Stalin* (Kampen: J. H. Kok, 1963), p. 62.
7. Marx, *Capital* I, Volksausgabe, p. 185f., and *Grundrisse*, p. 594, in Bottomore and Rubel, *Karl Marx: Selected Writings in Sociology and Social Philosophy* (London: Watts, 1963), pp. 88-91.
8. Marx, *Capital, I.* Volksausgabe, p. 188, in Bottomore and Rubel, *op. cit.*, p. 90.
9. (New York: Mentor, 1962).
10. *Ibid.,* p. 8.
11. *Ibid.,* p. 41.
12. *Ibid.,* pp. 44-45.

cultured relative, fire-making "memory man," or *Homo sapiens*.[13]

So too professors of history Wallbank and Taylor, in their *Civilization Past and Present*, state that a "universal cultural pattern" develops wherever man strives to cope with the interplay between his physical environment and human factors.[14] "Excavation in 1927–1929 near Peking," they inform us, "uncovered skeletal remains of . . . *Pithecanthropus pekinensis (Sinanthropus)*, or Peking Man. . . . *Pithecanthropus* fossils date back more than half a million years. . . . With Peking Man appears the first fossil evidence of human culture."[15]

"Irrespective of time and place," Wallbank and Taylor continue, "men have been following a pattern containing certain common elements such as social organization, political institutions, economic activities, law, science, art, religion, and philosophy. This has been termed the 'universal culture pattern.' When a group of people behave similarly and share the same institutions and ways of life, they can be said to possess the same culture. . . . When men no longer have to submit to brute necessity but begin to dominate their environment, they are at last in a position to remold their patterns of living, to create goods and values, and to transmit a common social heritage. When this process has continued to the point where men exert a wide control over nature and have developed a highly complex culture pattern, they can be said to possess a civilization."[14]

So much for the materialistic concept of culture and its origins. But even antimaterialistic idealists (especially in Germany)—though rejecting the materialistic view as to the animalistic origins of human culture in favor of a rather pantheistic one which stresses the essential unity or at least the very close affinity of God and man, have largely agreed with the materialists as to the comprehensive nature of human culture.

Culturological giants like Harnack, Meyer, Windelband, Natorp, Hinneberg, and Spengler have written comprehensive historical

---

13. *Ibid.*, pp. 46-49.
14. Chicago, Atlanta, Dallas, Palo Alto, Fair Lawn, N. J.: Scott, Foresman, 1960, pp. 7-8.
15. *Ibid.*, p. 25.

3

treatises—Windelband, for example, declaring: "Under 'culture' we understand the entirety of what the human consciousness produces from data."[16] Others again have perhaps rather less ambitiously written detailed and extensive monographs on the various *aspects* of culture, such as: on speech (thus Naumann), on art (thus Duorak), on painting (thus Burdach), on ideas (thus Korff), on music (thus Gurlitt), on education (thus Spranger), and on tribal affiliation (thus Nadler). And yet others have attempted to *subsume* culture under man's spirit (thus Sombart), his soul (thus Brüggemann), or his psyche (thus Jaspers).[17]

From a more holistic and at least semi-Christian viewpoint, Hugh Black characterizes culture as an attempt to promote man's welfare and to prevent his deterioration by seeking the full realization of his powers not by limitation, but by expansion, and by obeying his nature fearlessly. As such, culture carries with it the "sacred duty to develop *all* the faculties, to train the mind, to attempt to reach a *complete* and well balanced state of existence, to become *all* that it is possible for each individual to become."[18] And attempting to draw all these various idealistic threads together, Bornhäuser somewhat pantheistically concludes: "Culture is *the system of human activity,* which lays down a goal, acknowledges value, and attempts to supply goods," inasmuch as "culture is the culture of the soul (*Seelenkultur*), in which *nature and spirit* are indissolubly conjoined."[19]

Now all of these views are surely correct in generally seeing culture as embracing the total activity of man and in relating culture to the extension of man's dominion over his environment. But all of these views—both materialistic and idealistic—are faulty as regards their account of the origin and the essence of culture. Actually, only in the light of the Bible can we shed real light on the nature of culture, for, as the Psalmist of old confessed, "in Thy light shall we

---

16. As quoted in W. J. Aalders, *Reformatie en Cultuur,* in Wielenga, "Christendom en Cultuur," a chapter in his *Het Wezen van het Christendom* (Kampen: J. H. Kok, n.d.), p. 262, n. 7.

17. Cf. Wielenga, *op. cit.,* p. 257, n. 2.

18. *Culture and Restraint* (London: Hodder & Stoughton, 1901), p. 4.

19. Bornhäuser, "Kulturwissenschaft und Kulturphilosophie," in *Religion in Geschichte und Gegenwart.*

4

see the light" (Ps. 36:9). Consequently, it will be the purpose of this chapter to inquire of the origin and essence of culture—"What saith the Scriptures?" (Rom. 4:3). For inasmuch as the Bible alone can give us this information, it is to the Bible that we must now turn.

* * * * *

In this chapter on the roots of culture, then, we shall first seek to present the Biblical concept of culture. Second, we shall attempt to demonstrate how God is the Prime Author of all true culture. Third, we shall try to show how God appointed Adam to produce culture. Fourth, it will then be seen that Adam needed a humanity to help him to do this. Fifth, it will next be indicated how man's divine charter to develop culture is co-extensive with the whole of human history. And sixth, it will finally be claimed that only true cultural activity gives real meaning to human life itself.

* * * * *

First, then, what is the Biblical concept of culture? How does the Word of God define man's cultural activity?

The word "culture" is derived from the Latin *cultura,* meaning "cultivation," and it ultimately takes us back via the Latin Vulgate translation of the Scriptures to Adam's cult-ivation of the garden of Eden. Indeed, the first thing God ever told man to do was to "be fruitful, and multiply, and replenish the earth, and subdue it,"[20] which Adam started to do immediately after God "put him in the garden of Eden to dress it."[21] And this dressing of the garden constituted *culture,* yes, (horti-)*culture.*

Now this initial cultural activity of Adam was then performed not *humanitatis gratia,* not for the sake of his fellow man. After all, at that stage, Adam was still the only human being in the universe, so there was no other human person then in existence who could immediately be benefitted by Adam's cultural labors. For this reason, the humanistic doctrine of the essence of culture is clearly irreconcilable with Scripture.

Moreover, Adam attended to the garden in sole obedience to his

---

20. Gen. 1:28 cf. vs. 26; Gen. 9:7; Ps. 8 and Heb. 2.
21. Gen. 2:15; Heb. 6:7; James 3:3, 7, 12; 5:7.

5

Creator, solely to the glory of God, *soli Deo gratia*. For God had put him there specifically "to dress it,"[21] that is, to turn non-human 'nature' into human 'culture,' to turn the garden of *nature* into an exhibit of human horti-*culture*, to the glory of God. As the great dialectical theologian Karl Barth (with whom we often disagree!) has stated (in his 1926 Amsterdam lecture on "Church and Culture") human culture is to be viewed in relation "to its *theologischen Innenaspekt*" (or internal theological aspect); and in this respect Barth not without merit characterized culture as "the *Aufgabe* [or injunction] laid down in the Word of God to realize the destiny of man in the unity of soul and body."[22]

Now although culture should always and exclusively be undertaken to the glory of God alone, at the same time, however, *future humanity is also benefitted thereby,* inasmuch as not only Adam himself was advantaged by his cultivation of the garden, but also, at a later stage, his wife too. Moreover, had sin not intervened, all the future descendants of Adam and Eve would also have prospered as a result of early man's progressive cultivation of the land of Eden. Accordingly, the great Reformed exegete F. W. Grosheide is surely also correct where he (more accurately than Barth!) defines culture "as the *bezinksel* . . . *neergeslagen* [or deposited sublimate] remaining after a material and spiritual struggle, which becomes the possession of men of a certain period."[23]

The word "culture," then, as we have written elsewhere, aptly describes "the God-ordained result [or better: the God-ordained permanent deposit] of the total normative activity of man in his exploitation, classification and expression of the world outside of him and within him, built on the traditions of the past and constantly expanded for the use of present and future generations."[24]

And this, we would suggest, is a workable definition of the Biblical

---

22. Cf. Wielenga, *op. cit.*, pp. 259, 263n.
23. "Cultuur," in *Christelijke Encyclopaedie* (Kampen: J. H. Kok, 1925), I, 526.
24. Lee, *Culture: A Theological and Philosophical Analysis of the Origin, Spread and Goal of Culture* (Cape May, N. J.: Shelton College Press, 1967) p. 1.

concept of culture (a more extensive definition of which, however, we give in our appendix below).

*   *   *   *   *

Second, where does culture ultimately come from? What is the deepest root from which it is derived?

Now it must surely be admitted, at least by all Christians, that all culture, like everything else in the present world, has been defiled by sin (Gen. 3:17-18; Rom. 8:20-22). Hence, irrespective of whether it is practiced by dedicated Christians or by absolute infidels, all art, all poetry, all science, all philosophy (and, let us hasten to add, all theology too) displays the disfiguring marks of sin to a greater or lesser extent. Even the very ploughing of the wicked is evil (Prov. 21:4); whatsoever is not of faith, is sin (Rom. 14:23); and even all the righteousnesses of the people of God are but as filthy rags! (Isa. 64:6).

All culture, we say, is disfigured by sin to a greater or to a *lesser* extent. For in spite of the universal evidences of sin and its destructiveness, we are also surrounded by equally universal evidences of God and His goodness! Indeed, His graciousness ever overrides our sinfulness. This is true of all things, and hence of culture too. For God will never forsake the true work of His own hands (Ps. 138:8).

Yes, all true culture is in the final analysis the work of *God's* own hands, even though it is, of course, produced by God *through man's free agency*. For although all the imperfections in culture are exclusively a result of the *sins of men,* nevertheless all that is really good and true and pleasant in culture is a result solely of the *grace of God*. Indeed, and in spite of science falsely so-called (I Tim. 6:20) and false philosophy and vain deceit (Col. 2:9), it is God Who is the All-knowing Scientist and the All-wise Philosopher behind whatsoever things are really true (Phil. 4:8). For from God and through God and to God are *all* things (Rom. 11:36)—yes, all the "things" of culture too.

Indeed, "whatsoever things are true, whatsoever things are honest

7

or venerable,[25] whatsoever things are just, whatsoever things are pure, whatsoever things are lovely" (Phil. 4:8), are all from *God* (Rom. 11:36). In law, whatsoever things are truly just are from God, the Judge of all the earth (Gen. 18:25). In art, it is God Who is the Supreme Artist[26] of whatsoever things are lovely (Phil. 4:8)— for God flings His paint-pots against the canvas of the sky at every sunset (cf. Gen. 1:31), and it is God Who covers the wings of the dove with silver and her feathers with yellow gold (Ps. 68:13).

But the Lord God Almighty is not merely the Lord and Origin of all the humanitarian sciences such as philosophy and law and art. He is also the Lord and Origin of *all* culture. Hence, He is also the Lord and Origin of all the natural sciences as well. He is the Lord and Origin of all astronomy—He Who binds the Pleiades and Who can loosen the belt of Orion; He Who brings forth the twelve signs of the Zodiac in His own good time and Who guides the Great Bear (Job 38:31-32). He is the Lord and Origin of all meteorology—He Who is the Father of the rain, the Maker of the ice and the frost, the Freezer of the snow and the hail, the Driver of the wind and the clouds, and the Thrower of the lightning (Job 38:22-37). And He is the Lord and Origin of all geology—He Who is the Depositor and Preserver of the gold of Ophir and the topaz of Ethiopia (Job 28:16-23).

It is God Who is the Prime Architect and Master Builder, Who laid the foundations of the earth, Who laid the measures thereof, Who stretched the line upon it, and Who laid its corner stone (Job 38:4-6). God is the Supreme Musician, the Composer of the song of creation which the morning stars sang together when all of the sons of God shouted for joy (Job 38:7). And it is God, the Word of God, Who "lighteth every man that cometh into the world" (John 1:9); Who enlightens every scientist and philosopher and musician and artist that comes into the world (Ex. 35:21–36:2); and Who even

---

25. Cf. the Afrikaans (South African) Revised Version of Phil. 4:8, which correctly renders the original. Cf. too the *marginal* reading of the Authorized (King James) Version of the English Bible.
26. Prov. 8:30. Cf. chap. III, n. 16, below.

8

enlightens every parent respecting the giving of a name to every child that comes into the world (Eph. 3:14-15).

"Every *good* gift and *every* perfect gift is from above, and cometh down from the Father of lights!" (James 1:17). It is *God*, then, Who is the Primary Author of all true culture.

*　*　*　*　*

Third, however, God sovereignly and eternally decided to make *another* cult-ivator, though one subject to His guidance—namely, *man*.

Without divine *endowment,* man could cult-ivate nothing. "For God *giveth to man* that [which] is good in His sight—wisdom, and knowledge, and joy" (Eccles. 2:26). It is, then, only in a *secondary* sense that man can be described as the source of culture. In fact, man can cult-ivate and can be described as a cultural being at all only insofar as he somehow resembles that glorious Being, the great Culti-vator, the Lord God of culture. And this resemblance is best seen in the fact that man, the earthly lord of culture, was created as the likeness and image of God, the Supreme Lord of culture. Indeed, man is the very child, the very "offspring" of God (Gen. 1:26; Luke 3:38; Acts 17:28-29). And just as God had "cult-ivated" the world by manufacturing it in six divine working days, so too was man, God's image, to cult-ivate the world six days every week, down through all subsequent history. For God created nature. And from nature, man, as God's image, was now to "create" culture.

As the Second Helvetic Confession of sixteenth-century Protestant Switzerland declares, "Now concerning man, Scripture says that in the beginning he was made good according to the image and likeness of God; that God placed him in Paradise and made *all* things subject to him."[27] God the Father decreed to make man; God the Son spoke creatively to form man; and God the Spirit breathed into man the breath of life. The Three Persons of the Triune God took counsel with One Another and said, "Let Us make man in Our image, after Our likeness, and let them have dominion over the fish of the sea, and over the fowl of the air, and over the cattle, and over all the earth,

---

27. *Second Helvetic Confession,* chap. VII.

9

and over every creeping thing that creepeth upon the earth!" "So God created . . . them. And God blessed them, and God said unto them: 'Be fruitful, and multiply, and replenish the earth, and subdue it; and have dominion over the fish of the sea, and over the fowl of the air, and over every living thing that moveth upon the earth!' " (Gen. 1:26-28).

Now the above Biblical quotation (which the New Scofield Reference Bible well describes as "the divine *magna charta* for all true scientific and material progress," and which we shall accordingly call the "great charter" of dominion or the "dominion charter") was the first command ever given by God to man. It was the very first sound that ever thundered into man's ears as soon as he had taken his very first breath, and it is clear that the fact that man was created as the image of God implies a whole host of cultural possibilities. For man was to cultivate and to subdue the world, to replenish the earth, to dominate the sea and the air and the land. Under God, he was, as the Scots Confession of 1560 states, given "lordship" over creation[28] and thus appointed under God as the vice president of the universe, as it were, in order to lord it over the entire earth and all its fullness. And, in exercising this dominion, man was destined to fulfill a vast host of cultural tasks.

What a fascinating variety of *cultural* duties man was to perform! He was to subdue the earth—an agri-cultural task (Gen. 1:28; 2:15). He was to cult-ivate the friendship of his wife—a socio-cultural task (Gen. 2:18, 23-24). He was to tend to all the plants and flowers— a horti-cultural task (Gen. 1:29-30; 2:15). He was to cultivate bees and horses, as in api-culture and equi-culture. He was to cultivate himself, as in physical culture and voice culture. And every sabbath day he was to rest from all his manifold tasks and worship his Maker —a liturgical cult-ic task (Gen. 1:29–2:3; cf. Ex. 20:8-11).

These and many other tasks (mentioned below) were required by God of man. God was the Lord of all culture, and He required that man, as His own image, should reflect that culture. So God incorporated all these cultural tasks into the covenant of works (Hosea

---

28. *The Scots Confession of 1560*, chap. II.

10

6:7, margin) which He made with Adam and all Adam's descendants.[29] It is true that Adam was created with *unloseable, everlasting existence*. Once he had been created as the very image of the everlasting God, Adam could not lose his own everlasting, continued existence, and so he would never be annihilated. But the blessed life or happiness which Adam was given before the fall could be lost. In that latter case, Adam would receive the curse of death and *end up in hell or everlasting misery*. For in order to continue in his first estate of *losable blessedness* and to increase it until it would ultimately have been translated into *unlosable blessedness,* it was necessary for Adam *to keep the covenant of works* and *to execute his cultural tasks.*

If and when Adam and his descendants had performed all these manifold tasks faithfully, and thereby kept God's moral law, they would thereby ultimately have earned *unlosable* blessedness or everlasting *life* (Gen. 3:22 cf. Rev. 2:7) as a permanent reward—for the Ten Commandments (Ex. 20:1-16; Deut. 5:6-21), written on Adam's heart (Eccles. 7:29; 3:11; Rom. 2:14-22), not only warned him against transgression (Rom. 7:7; I John 3:4), but also *required* him to labor and to be disciplined and to promote life and to multiply and to replenish the earth and to earn his bread honestly and to *develop culture* (Ex. 20:7-11 and cf. n. 36 below).

However, if Adam and his descendants[30] tried to evade all cultural effort by taking a short cut to gain that knowledge, by attempting to steal the utmost knowledge by eating of the forbidden fruit of the tree of the knowledge of good and evil—which they in fact did—they would then lose even *that* measure of life or blessedness with which

---

29. Hos. 6:7, Revised Version, cf. Authorized Version *margin*. Cf. **Rom.** 2:14, 15 and 5:12ff.; cf. Gen. 1:26 (". . . let them . . .") and Gen. 3:20 (". . . mother of *all* living . . ."). Cf. too Diemer, *Het Scheppingsverbond met Adam* (Kampen: J. H. Kok); Donald MacLeod, "Federal Theology—an Oppressive Legalism?", in *Banner of Truth* magazine (Edinburgh, Feb. 1974); Lee, *The Covenantal Sabbath* (London: Lord's Day Observance Society, [n.d.] 1972); *Westminster Confession of Faith*, VII:1-3; *Westminster Larger Catechism*, Q. 20-22; and cf. the text at notes 35-36 below.

30. Fve, of course, is also a descendant of Adam, her federal head, I Cor. 11:12.

.

11

they were created (Gen. 2:7, 17 cf. Eph. 4:24 and Col. 3:11) and suffer agony for ever, *even though they could never cease to exist.*

One thing that Adam and his descendants could never lose even after the fall, however—at least as long as they continued to exist here on earth after sinning and prior to their deaths and burials—was the capacity to *work.* Man's labors could indeed become greatly burdened by sin—which they did! (Gen. 3:19)—but his cultural tasks as such would always remain and beckon him even after the fall to come and perform them. For even fallen man in some sense remained and still remains the (now broken!) image of the Lord God of culture (Gen. 9:6-7; James 3:7, 9).

*   *   *   *   *

Fourth, then, all men are to be engaged in cultural activity, for all men are covenantally obliged to obey God's commands to Adam.

It has been stated above that the Adamitic covenant of cultural works was made with all of Adam's future descendants no less than it was made with Adam himself. For in Adam as its federal head and legal representative, all mankind is obligated to keep and execute this covenant.[29] And indeed, Adam *could* never have fulfilled the covenant by discharging all those cultural tasks by himself alone—he *needed* a humanity to help him to do so! For although these tasks sound so easy by virtue of the very simplicity with which they are described in the Genesis account, in actual fact they embrace every possible aspect of all human endeavor.

Adam's own personal agricultural task, for example, only started by cultivating the garden of Eden in all simplicity (Gen. 2:15)—yet in Adam as its federal head, all mankind was required to develop every acre, to subdue the entire earth (Gen. 1:28). Adam's own nautical task commenced with merely asserting his authority over a few fish—but mankind was and is ultimately destined to achieve total dominion over all the world's oceans, to become king of the sea and all its fullness (Ex. 20:8-11). Adam's own engineering tasks were originally to collect gold and bdellium and the onyx stone—but under mankind this was to develop to embrace the construction of gigantic mines and factories and automobiles throughout the world (Gen. 2:11-12; Job 28). Man's military task was initially simply to keep

12

he garden, that is, to guard it against the intrusion of sin and the devil[31]—but after the advent of sin, this task was ultimately to embrace all the armies of soldiers, doctors, and policemen throughout all ages in the entire world, guarding the interests of mankind and fighting against the consequences of sin and the works of the devil.

The unfolding of the world's culture is thus the task of all humanity—by virtue of all humanity's involvement in the Adamitic covenant of works.

In the command to have dominion over the land (Gen. 1:28), we are commissioned to operate tractors and trucks and automobiles. In the command to have dominion over the air (Gen. 1:28), we find the germ of all aeronautics—of airplanes, rockets, and sputnik satellites. In the command to have dominion over the sea (Gen. 1:28), we are enjoined to construct great ocean liners and bathoscopes and submarines and to farm the ocean beds. In the command to have dominion over the cattle and beasts of the earth (Gen. 1:28), we have the blueprint of all cattle ranching, sheepfarming, and livestock husbandry. The command to exploit the creeping thing (Gen. 1:28) naturally includes the silkworm and the rock lobster, and hence points us to the development of the rock lobster trade and the silk industry. And in the reference to man's task of giving names to all the animals (Gen. 2:19), we find the germ of all the natural sciences as represented by zoology.

Truly, Adam could never undertake all these tasks alone! And neither was this expected of him. As has already been stated, when God made the covenant of works with Adam, He made it with all of Adam's descendants as well. This is one of the chief reasons why God commanded man to "multiply and replenish the earth, and subdue it" (Gen. 1:28). For Adam could never subdue it alone. Only by multiplying could man subdue the earth—namely, subdue it in and through his descendants. So God committed these tremendous tasks of developing the world's culture to all mankind; to every

---

31. Gen. 2:15: ". . . to guard it [the garden]," cf. the Hebrew lĕshômrāḥ, from the verb shāmar, "to guard." Cf. the noun shōmēr, "a policeman," in modern Hebrew. Cf. too Kuyper, *De Leer der Verbonden* (Kampen: J. H. Kok, 1909), p. 51.

13

scientist, every farmer, every technician, every teacher, every house-wife—to every one of *us!*[24]

For, like Adam's, our cultural task too is enormous! We are to dominate and therefore also to count and to measure the fowl and the fish and every living thing—a mathematical task. We are to move out into the world and to replenish or fill the whole earth—a spatial as well as a mechanical (or movemental) task. We are to subdue and to have dominion over the earth (a physical task), over the plants (a botanical task), and over the animals (a zoological task). And we are also to react to our own natural feelings, such as our desire for a mate, as Adam did when he saw the animals pairing off together—a psychical task (Gen. 1:28-29; 2:18-25).

Furthermore, we are to pursue logic, as Adam did—when, for example, he reflected on the differences between the various kinds of trees. We are to make history, as we multiply and fill the earth and have dominion over it. We are to develop languages, as we like Adam give names to animals and plants. And we are to expand our social lives in our companionship with one another, as Adam did with Eve (Gen. 1:26-29; 2:18-25).

Moreover, we are to practice economics, as Adam did in his exploitation of gold and bdellium and the onyx stone. We are to develop the arts, as Adam did when he dressed the garden of Eden. We are to cultivate the discipline of law, as Adam did when he kept the garden safe from the illegal transgression of the devil. We are to develop our ethical abilities, as Adam did when he loved his wife. And we are to fear God and to keep His commandments pistically or faithfully (Eccles. 12:13), as Adam did in his original uprightness *coram Deo* or in the constant presence of God (Eccles. 7:29).

All this, however, is a task of all tasks—a task so huge that it requires the joint efforts of all men everywhere—of Adam and his children and our children and grandchildren and the whole of mankind! For even all mankind would take many thousands of years to complete all these tremendous tasks. For just as God the Lord of culture had created the raw materials of the universe during that humanly immeasurable period of time prior to the first day (Gen.

14

1:1-2), and thereafter had proceeded to fashion the earth from those raw materials during the succeeding world week (Gen. 1:31)—so too did and does man take the God-given raw materials of culture to hand, and he then proceeded and still proceeds to fashion or make the world's cultural treasures from that raw material. Proceeds to fashion—a process of many thousands of years! For man will never cease from his tremendous cultural activities until the end of history, until the vast time-lapse of God's world-week and its still-continuing seventh-day sabbath—the day without an evening![32]—has yielded to the final advent of God's eighth day, the day of the Lord.[33]

* * * * *

Fifth, then, man's cultural obligations endure until the very end of history, as long as man is here on earth.

And so "God created man in His own image, . . . and God blessed them, and God said [through His Son or *Word!*—John 1:1, 14] unto them: 'Be fruitful, and multiply, and replenish the earth, and subdue it . . . !' " "And on the seventh day, God ended His work which He had made; and He rested on the seventh day from all His work which He had made. And God blessed the seventh day and sanctified it: Because that in it He had rested from all His work which God created, *to make it.*"[34]

God had just created the world and all its inhabitants, created the raw materials for the further development of culture. And with the creation of man just prior to the commencement of God's seventh-day sabbath, the Lord ended His work of perfect creation. Henceforth God would still continue to preserve and to develop the existing

---

32. Gen. 2:1-3. Unlike the preceding six days, the seventh day here has no "evening," implying that it did not then end, but was left open, continuing down through the subsequent centuries, cf. Heb. 4:3-11. Cf. Lee, *The Covenantal Sabbath*, pp. 36ff., 56-58, etc.

33. Mal. 3:16–4:5; cf. John 20:1, 19, 26 and I Cor. 15:16, 20, 22 and Acts 17:31. Cf. too Lee, *The Covenantal Sabbath.*

34. Gen. 1:26–2:3, *margin.* The Hebrew Kal infinitivus constructus *la'ăsôth* probably here expresses purpose, cf. Hab. 1:8 (". . . as the eagle that hasteth *to eat* [*lĕ'êcōl*]"). On Gen. 2:3, cf. especially Kuyper, *Van de Voleinding* (Kampen: J. H. Kok, 1929), I, 24. Cf. too especially Heb. 4: 3-11.

raw material; but henceforth He would make or manufacture or fashion nothing new, nothing additional. No new basic kind of creature would God ever again create (John 5:16-18). With the creation of man on the sixth day as the crown and lord of creation, God had finished creating (Gen. 1:26–2:3). Now God rests from creation. Rests in man, the masterpiece of His creation. In man, God sabbaths from creation, in order "to make it,"[34] to fashion it. And God appoints man His masterpiece to make it for Him. He delegates His exclusive right to make things to man as His deputy, as His image. God shows to man the created earth, and it is as if He says: "Subdue it! I have created the world *to make it—to make it through YOU.* I have made you, *now YOU must make the earth.* I shall rest on this sabbath of creation week until the end of history. And I shall watch how you develop and subdue the earth and make it for Me. I shall watch how you proceed with the development of culture. And I shall hold you accountable on My eighth day, on the Day of the Lord at the end of history!"

As we read in the Westminster Confession: "The first covenant made with man was a covenant of works, wherein life was promised to Adam, and in him to his posterity, upon condition of perfect and personal obedience."[35] As we read in the Westminster Larger Catechism: "The providence of God toward man in the estate in which he was created, was, the placing him in paradise, appointing him to dress it, giving him liberty to eat of the fruit of the earth, putting the creatures under his dominion, and ordaining marriage for his help affording him communion with Himself, instituting the Sabbath, entering into a covenant of life with him, upon condition of personal, perfect, and perpetual obedience, of which the tree of life was a pledge; and forbidding to eat of the tree of knowledge of good and evil, upon the pain of death."[36] And as we read in the Belgic Confession: "We believe that the Father, by the Word, that is, by His Son, hath created of nothing, the heaven, the earth, and all creatures as it seemed good unto Him; giving unto each creature its being,

35. *Westminster Confession of Faith,* VII:2.
36. *Westminster Larger Catechism,* Q. 20.

shape, form and several offices to serve its Creator; that He doth also still uphold and govern them by His eternal providence, and infinite power, for the service of mankind, to the end that man may serve his God."[37]

*   *   *   *   *

Sixth, it should by now be realized that human life in all ages accordingly has no real meaning apart from cultural activity.

"What profit has the man who works at that in which he labours?" asks the Preacher (Eccles. 1:3). "I have seen the travail, which God hath given to the sons of man to be exercised in it. God hath made every thing beautiful in His time. Also, He hath set the world in their heart, so that no man can find out the work that God maketh from the beginning to the end" (Eccles. 3:9-11).

God has set the world in the heart of man—the world of art, the world of science, the world of music, the world of philosophy—the whole world and all its cultural fullness! Every one of us has the potential of the whole world in his heart—the God-given ability to grasp the meaning of culture, and to picturize cultural events in their progress through world history. And therefore, as the Preacher again tells us, "It is well for a man to rejoice, and to do good in his life. And also that every man should eat and drink, and enjoy the good of all his labour, it is the gift of God." (Eccles 3:12-13). For, "It is good and comely for one to eat and to drink, and to enjoy the good of all his labour that he taketh under the sun all the days of his life, which God giveth him: for it is his portion. Every man also to whom God hath given riches and wealth, and hath given him power to eat thereof, and to take his portion, and to rejoice in his labour; this is the gift of God" (Eccles. 5:18-19).

And inasmuch as godly labor and godly family living and godly culture are all intertwined in the dominion charter, the Preacher correctly also advises us: "Live joyfully with the wife whom thou lovest all the days of the life of thy vanity, which He hath given thee under the sun, all the days of thy vanity: for that is thy portion in this life, and in thy labour which thou takest under the sun. Whatso-

---

37. *Belgic Confession,* art. XII.

ever thy hand findeth to do, do it with thy might!" (Eccles. 9:9-10).

Indeed, as the apostle Paul later remarked: "Whether therefore ye eat, or drink, or whatsoever ye do, do all to the glory of God!" (I Cor. 10:31).

*　　*　　*　　*　　*

We summarize.

In this chapter on the roots of culture, we first saw that even non-Christian scholars such as leading materialists and idealists, although respectively assuming an ultimately animalistic or otherwise a pantheistic origin of human culture, did nevertheless correctly see it as the result of the total activity of man in dominating his environment.

Second, it was seen that the Bible itself stresses the primary importance of the God-centered character of true culture, and only secondarily stresses the importance of cultural benefits to the human community and to future generations.

Third, it was realized that all true culture is grounded in God, Who from previously created raw materials "cult-ivated" the world in six divine working days.

Fourth, it was shown how God endowed man, as His image, with cultural abilities to dominate the earth and the sea and the sky under His guidance.

Fifth, we saw that Adam could never culturally dominate the whole world all alone, but that he needed all his many descendants to help him to do this.

Sixth, it was shown that man is to be involved in cultural activity down through all the ages, and will finally be rewarded or punished for this activity at the end of history on the Day of the Lord.

And seventh, it was seen that life in all ages is devoid of real significance without at least some cultural interests.

*　　*　　*　　*　　*

What, then, is the importance of the aforegoing to man's cultural activities *today?*

First, we are to recognize the inescapability of culture, permeating as it does every facet of human activity. The question, then, is not *whether* we shall become involved in cultural activity—for *that* is unavoidable! The question is rather: With *which* kind of cultural activity are we involved—god*ly* culture, or god*less* culture?

Second, we should reject both the materialistic and the idealistic accounts of the origin and essence of culture. For culture did not first develop among pre-human higher primates, nor is culture simply the activity of some or other Universal World-Idea pantheistically emanating from the assumed divinity of man. Even though animals too do make things, and even though the Triune God is the ultimate Author of all true culture, cultural activity is essentially the normative response of *man* (as God's image) to the Lord's injunction that man dominate the world to the glory of God.

And third, we are to know that all of our labors—whether they be mathematical, mechanical, physical, biological, psychological, analytical, historical, social, economic, aesthetic, legal, ethical, or cultic—are all essentially cultural activities of a religious nature performed *coram Deo* or in the presence of the one true Triune God Who rewards or retards us accordingly here and now in this present life, and Who will ultimately also recompense us in the next life either with everlasting bliss or with everlasting punishment!

*   *   *   *   *

So all men—even materialists and idealists—see the fact of culture, the lock, as it were. But only the believer—the Christian—has the key to this lock—the key which opens the door to the origin and essence and goal of culture. David sought this key when he inquired: "O Lord our Lord. . . . When I consider Thy heavens, the work of Thy fingers, the moon and the stars which Thou hast ordained—what is man, that Thou art mindful of him?" And David found the key to man's existence when he exclaimed: "Thou has made him a little lower than a divine being, and hast crowned him with glory and honour. Thou madest him to have dominion over the works of Thy hands—Thou hast put all things under his feet; all sheep and oxen, yea, and the beasts of the field; the fowl of the air, and the fish of the sea, and whatsoever passeth through the paths of the sea" (Ps. 8:1-8).

What is true culture? True culture is the work of man to the glory of God. And what is man? Man is just a little less than a divine being. He is the very image of God. He is destined to dominate the earth. But in so doing, he must not forget the Lord God Who created the heavens, the moon, and the stars. Man is the lord of culture only because he is the image of the God of culture. For the Origin of man and the Root of all his true culture is the Lord God, the Maker of heaven and earth.

II

THE GROWTH OF CULTURE

How did culture spread, once it had come into being? What was the pattern of its early expansion?

The Marxists inform us that man, after evolving from the ape, undergoes six successive stages of growth (namely, 'primitive communism,' slavery, feudalism, capitalism, socialism, and future communism),[1] and that after "gold and silver, . . . [and] iron and corn . . . civilized man and ruined the human race,"[2] ('primitive communistic') culture became transformed into slave culture not later than about 1500 B.C., which slavery generally lasted until after the beginning of the Christian era. Under 'primitive communism' man had used only fire and stones, had labored only in food-gathering and hunting and livestock-farming, had been organized only into clans, had lived only in communal longhouses, had possessed no government nor money, and had existed in general as did the Poly-

---

1. Cf. Lee, *Communist Eschatology: A Christian Philosophical Analysis of the Post-Capitalistic Views of Marx, Engels, and Lenin* (Nutley, N. J.: The Craig Press, 1974), p. 43, notes 45-58. In this connection, cf. especially, (1) Marx, *A Contribution to the Critique of Political Economy*, Preface, pp. 10-13, in Burns, *Handbook of Marxism* (London: Victor Gollancz, 1935), pp. 371-373; (2) Engels, *The Origin of the Family, Private Property, and the State* (Moscow: Foreign Languages Publishing House, n.d.); and (3) Lenin, *Materialism and Empirio-Criticism* (London: Lawrence and Wishart, 1927), p. 325f., and *The State*, in *Selected Works*, XI, p. 644, in Bochenski and Niemeyer, *Handbuch des Weltkommunismus* (Freiburg/Munich: Karl Alber, 1958), pp. 34-35.

2. Engels, *Anti-Dühring*, p. 156, cf. *The Origin of the Family*, in Acton, *The Illusion of the Epoch: Marxism-Leninism as a Philosophical Creed* (London: Cohen & West, 1962), p. 136.

nesians right down to the last century. However, with the growth of human culture from 'primitive communism' into slavery, men began to use iron and to make boats, to labor as potters and weavers and smelters, to live in city states, to practice slavery, to set up government under chieftains, to use gold and silver as money, and generally to exist in a way much the same as did the ancient Romans.[3]

The Californian educationalists Rogers and Adams and Brown are even more specific. According to them, after first the Neanderthal culture and then the Cromagnon culture had passed from the scene of history,[4] *Homo sapiens* appeared, and differentiated into Caucasians, Negroes, and Mongolians,[5] each race with its own culture. Writing and metal-smelting, they believe, were first developed considerably before 3000 B.C., so that by that time civilization had already dawned.[6] Under these various ancient civilized cultures, man "was master of the land, and had learned to work with nature. He had settled down in various fertile regions of the earth," (namely, in Mesopotamia, Palestine, and Egypt in the Eastern Hemisphere and later in the Panamanian isthmus in Mexico and Guatemala in the Western Hemisphere).[6]

According to the evolutionist Calder's *After the Seventh Day,* the civilized culture of *Homo sapiens* first grew up in the Persian plateau. Painted pottery emerged at Jericho in Palestine, on the caravan route between the ancient Egyptian culture and the culture of Mesopotamia or the land "between the rivers" of the Tigris and the Euphrates[7] (which, we are told in the Bible, originally flowed from the land of Eden—Gen. 2:10-11). And according to Calder's fellow evolutionists, the historians Wallbank and Taylor, the world's first civilized culture (embracing sowing, drainage, crafts, trade, smelting, writing, storing, wheeling, and sailing—and, at a somewhat later stage, also embracing architecture, law, mathematics, astrono-

---

3. Cf. Lee, *Communist Eschatology,* pp. 44-48, and especially the diagram on p. 45.
4. Rogers, Adams, Brown, *Story of Nations* (New York: Henry Holt, 1945), pp. 11-19.
5. *Ibid.,* pp. 19-20.
6. *Ibid.,* p. 23.
7. Page 71f.

my, and literature) grew up precisely in "the Tigris-Euphrates delta,"[8] whence it steadily spread further afield.

* * * * *

Such views as the above, although containing some elements of truth on account of the operation of God's common revelation and common grace, nevertheless need to be re-interpreted in the light of the infallible Bible. Accordingly, in this chapter on the growth of culture, we will endeavor to present the Scriptural view of the growth of early civilization (while reserving a more detailed discussion of the precise relationship between culture and civilization for our appendix below). Here, first we will discuss the very possibility of the development of culture after the fall. Second, we shall trace the growth of culture between the fall and the flood. Third, we shall consider the impact of the Noachic covenant on the further development of culture. Fourth, the influence of developing nationality on early culture must be noted. Fifth, we shall consider the development of culture in pre-exilic Israel. And sixth, we shall indicate the importance of the old world culture between the Old Testament and New Testament dispensations.

* * * * *

First, then, God Himself made it possible for man's culture to develop, even after and in spite of the fall.

In his initial act of willful rebellion against God, man lazily tried to evade the tremendous cultural efforts required if he were obediently to execute the covenant of works to the glory of God. For, by stealing the forbidden fruit of the tree of the knowledge of good and evil, man ingloriously sought to attain to unlosable everlasting life *immediately* (Gen. 3:4, 5, 22), instead of earning it *ultimately* as a reward for patiently executing his own cultural tasks to the glory of God, as he had been commanded to do (Gen. 1:28; Heb. 4:4, 11; Rev. 14:13). Thus man deliberately disturbed the harmonious and peaceful development of the world's culture.

As a result of one irresponsible act, man invited a catastrophe which shattered the bliss of Eden and of the entire earth. And in-

---

8. *Op. cit.*, pp. 36-42.

stead of continuing to develop his God-given works of culture harmoniously and gradually acquiring more knowledge, man tried to desert his divinely ordained cultural tasks and take a forbidden short cut to that knowledge by illegally eating of the forbidden tree (Gen. 2:17; 3:11, 19). In so doing, man became radically evil.[9] Instead of remaining a faithful covenant-keeper and continuing to live (cf. Gen. 6:18; 17:7), Adam transgressed the covenant and became a covenant-breaker and died (Hos. 6:7 margin; Jer. 34:18)—and *in* Adam and *like* Adam all his descendants broke the covenant too (Rom. 5:12f.; Isa. 24:5). Moreover, as a result of the fall and the degradation of man as the lord of creation, creation itself became distorted and twisted, so that unregenerate man has now become subject to the wrath of God (John 3:36; Rom. 1:18); and the whole creation—including culture, the work of fallen man's hands (Gen. 6:5; Ps. 14)—has now become subjected to the bondage of corruption (Rom. 8:20-21).

Yet although mankind now became dead in sin (Eph. 2:1), God did not permit man to die outright, to die the second death at once.[10] For if man had been allowed to die fully right there and then, culture would have died with him. If man had died, Jesus Christ the son of Adam and the Seed of the woman could never have been born at all. Indeed, it was God's gracious purpose to save Adam and an elect part of his descendants; save them by the sacrificial merits of Jesus Christ substituted as a second Adam in their place. Adam and his culture, then, must not die, but live!

Adam, then, must not die! Hence, immediately after the fall, God intervened to save man and his culture—including even the soon-to-develop culture of Cain and the ungodly Cainites! (Gen. 4:20-24). And this God did when He promised to send the Seed of the woman to save elect mankind, to be bruised unto death by the devilish serpent, to die on Calvary for the sins of Adam and his elect descendants, to die so that elect mankind might live. God promised that. God gave His Word. The Word of God, God the Son Himself,

---

9. Gen. 5:3 cf. 6:5; 8:21; cf. Job 14:4.; Rom. 5:21f.
10. Gen. 2:17 cf. 5:4-5 and Rev. 21:8.

guaranteed that He personally would ultimately come down to earth and fulfill this promise!

It was the Word of God, the preexistent Christ Himself, Who guaranteed this promise immediately after the fall, and Who sustained this promise ever since and until He fulfilled it in His own incarnation, when He the Second Adam would graciously step into the shoes of the first Adam and be punished for the latter's breach of the covenant of works and Himself keep it and thus earn everlasting life for His children, and then donate that everlasting life to them in the covenant of grace (Isa. 42:1, 6). And God's first act to ratify this promise of the sacrificial death of the coming Seed of the woman, the coming Lamb of God, was probably His demonstration of the sacrificial death of a lamb when He made coats of animal skins for our first parents, and clothed them with the righteousness of the coming Lamb of God, as it were. For Adam and Eve were not to die, but to live! That Adam believed the promise of the coming Seed of the woman, believed the living Word of God, is indicated by the fact that he called his wife Eve—"the mother of all *living*." That Eve believed the promise is evidenced by the fact that she optimistically called her first-born son Cain—"I have gotten a man—*the Lord.*" For she erroneously though by expectant faith thought Cain to be the promised Lord and Savior, "the Seed of the woman."[11]

Adam and Eve, then, both believed in the coming Savior, were saved, and lived.[12] And their dying culture revived *with* them!

Man was immediately saved by believing the promise of the Word of God. But culture too was rescued, directly after the fall. The death of man would have caused the death of culture also, but the salvation of man implies the salvation of culture too. Culture too was saved, for Adam now left Eden, left together with Eve, "the mother of all living," the ancestral mother of the living Savior, the living Seed of the woman. They left Eden in order to multiply, in order to replenish the earth, and to subdue it—to multiply even unto the birth of the Seed of the woman, the Lord Jesus Christ, Who would

---

11. Gal. 3:15; cf. Gal. 4:4-6 and Gen. 3:15 & 4:1, margin, Hebrew: "Qānîthî 'îsh eth Jĕhôvāh."
12. Gen. 3:15 cf. 4:1, 25; 5:29; I Cor. 15:45-47; Gal. 3:27-29; John 1:29.

Himself save and replenish the earth and subdue it as never before.

Culture thus continued after the fall, for the Spirit of the promised Seed of the woman, the Spirit of the Word of God, continued to rule man, to strive with man, even though he had become flesh, had become mortal. For, "it is the Spirit in man, and the inspiration of the Almighty Who gives man understanding" (Gen. 6:3; Job 32:8), and "it is the Spirit that beareth witness, for the Spirit is truth" (I John 5:6). Culture thus continued, for God the Father, the First Person of the Trinity, continued to sustain the universe in spite of the curse on creation (John 5:17); and even immediately after the fall and for ever since until His own incarnation, the Second Person of the Trinity or the Word of God continued to sustain His saving promise— the promise of His future incarnation as the coming Seed of the woman; and the Third Person of the Trinity or the Spirit of God (the Spirit of the Word of God) continued to strive with man, and to rule man and his culture. Without the Word of God's promise of the Seed of the woman, without the rulings and strivings of the Spirit of God, fallen man and all his culture would have perished instantly! For, *"The day* that thou eatest, thou shalt die."[13] But the continuing life of man and of his culture after the fall was immediately and graciously guaranteed by the promised Word of God, and graciously ruled by the striving Spirit of God—so culture continued!

As the Decrees of Dordt of the Reformed Churches inform us, "There remain, however, in man, since the fall, the glimmerings of natural light, whereby he retains some knowledge of God, of natural things, and of the difference between good and evil, and discovers some regard for virtue and for maintaining an orderly external deportment."[14] For although "common grace" and "the light of nature" cannot *save* fallen man, nevertheless they do imply the *useful* exercise of "the gifts still left him after the fall."[15]

*   *   *   *   *

Second, we should note the growth of human culture between the fall and the flood.

---

13. Gen. 2:17; 3:11, 19 cf. Eph. 1:4-7; I Pet. 1:19-20; Rev. 13:8.
14. *Decrees of Dordt*, III & IV, 4.
15. *Ibid.*, III & IV, rejection of error 5.

Now it is true that man's cultural tasks were henceforth to be accomplished in the sweat of his face. Yet the institution of cultural labor continued even after the fall. God's cultural command was no more withdrawn after the fall than were the other pre-fall realities of the institution of marriage and the institution of the sabbath—which, of course, continued, in spite of sinful man's now total inability to use them solely to God's glory, but which God still justly expects him to do. Similarly, culture too continued and still continues, for even fallen man could not and cannot *but* develop culture; for the Spirit of the Lord God of culture strives within every man. Man is indestructibly a cultural being, and so he cannot help but search for the reason for his existence and the very meaning of life itself. And man searches for this meaning of life in science, in art, in philosophy—in culture! So, driven by the strivings of the Spirit of the Lord of culture, all sinful fallen men thirsted after culture (and still do today!) without knowing why!

Yet after the fall of man, his cultural tasks—which should have been a joy—now became increasingly onerous. The cursed ground which he was required to cultivate now became less productive, and required much toil and sweat to make it bear adequate fruits (Gen. 3:17-19). The further development of the humanitarian and natural sciences which God required of man, now became greatly hindered both by the curse of God on creation and by the limitations of human understanding (which had now become darkened as a result of sin).[16] Henceforth, long, drawn-out hours of tiresome and laborious effort were necessary, just to be able to keep alive. After spending the whole day hunting game or collecting food, not much time was left to develop and enjoy poetry and art and music! Life was a struggle. Fallen man had become primitive man; man the hunter (like Nimrod), man the food-collector (like Cain), man the herdsman (like Abel).[17]

Some men became nomadic, and wandered about traveling vast distances in search of game and food, as well as to escape from their

---

16. Gen. 3:17; Rom. 8:20-22; Eph. 4:18; Tit. 1:15; 3:3.
17. Gen. 4:3, 22 cf. 6:4 and 10:9.

enemies—much as do the Bushmen of South Africa's Kalahari and Namib deserts even today. We have a picture of this nomadic style of living in the history of the first man born after the fall. For Cain himself declared: "I shall be a fugitive and a vagabond in the earth, and it shall come to pass, that every one that findeth me, shall slay me" (Gen. 4:14). If Cain *had* been slain, however, the spread of that part of the world's culture which was destined to be developed by Cain's descendants (and from which Noah may well have profited to build the ark) would have been halted! And so the Lord God of culture graciously protected the nomad Cain from all his enemies (Gen. 4:15).

When nomadic man had found an area fertile enough to support a regular crop, however, he would settle down and establish a more permanent habitation in such a place. The degree of permanent residence there would necessitate better shelter, better water supplies and food storage, and better weapons for protection against enemies. In this way settlements would develop into villages, and villages into towns and cities.

So it is that we read that the nomad Cain "dwelt in the land of Nod [which word means 'to be on the move']" [18] . . . and he builded a city, and he called the name of the city after the name of his son—Enoch" (Gen. 4:17).

Now this "city of Enoch" which Cain built was, of course, certainly no modern metropolis. To start with, it probably consisted only of a few permanent dwellings surrounded by a wall of wooden stakes to protect the settlement against enemies and wild animals [19]—much like the log cabins and forts of the early American pioneers—or perhaps even rather more closely resembling the primitive American Indian settlements of old. And yet this primitive "city of Enoch" was nevertheless the germ of all modern cities and all contemporary culture and technology! For its degree of community life, of specialized trades, of communal protection, and of social cooperation,

18. Gen. 4:16; Hebrew *nod*, from the verb *nōd*, "to stray," and from the noun *nād*, "a fugitive."
19. Cf. F. L. Bakker, *Geschiedenis der Godsopenbaring—Oude Testament* (Kampen: J. H. Kok, 1955), and Gen. 4:17.

gave the inhabitants of that city a measure of spare time for the development of culture, just as the stake fence or city wall gave them a measure of security from enemies and wild beasts. Indeed, it is in precisely such an environment that one would expect to find culture developing—in a setting where one man could become the full-time farmer without having to make his own plowshare, and another could become the full-time blacksmith without having to collect his own food, and where both could supply one another's needs in an atmosphere of mutual interdependence and common benefit.

Hence we read that the descendants of Cain, all living in the city of Enoch, each had his own trade, his own cultural speciality. "Jabal . . . was the father of such as dwell in tents, and of such as have cattle. And his brother's name was Jubal: he was the father of all such as handle the harp and organ. And . . . Tubal-Cain, [he was] an instructor of every artificer in brass and iron" (Gen. 4:20-22).

Jabal was not only the father of all cattle-ranchers (and hence the pioneer of all livestock and agricultural technology), but we also read that he was in addition the father of all tent-dwellers (and hence the pioneer of all architecture). Furthermore, as tents may be made either from animal skins or woven from vegetable materials, Jabal was probably also a weaver (and, as such, the pioneer of the clothing industry). And, as Abraham Kuyper pointed out, Jabal conceivably slaughtered his sheep to obtain the necessary wool for the manufacture of woolen goods as textiles as well.[20]

Jubal was the first to use the harp (a percussion instrument) and the organ (a wind instrument). As his name implies, he was the pioneer of all "jubilation" and of all music. It is here where we must seek the germ of all symphonic concerts and all operatic performances, of all songs, and of all vocal accompaniment.

Closely connected with songs and vocal accompaniment, are ballads and poetry. Of these we already had a clear example in the marriage lyric of Adam when he first beheld Eve—"This is now bone

20. Kuyper, *Pro Rege* (Kampen: J. H. Kok, 1911), I, 190.

of my bones, and flesh of my flesh: she shall be called 'Woman,' because she was taken out of 'Man' " (Gen. 2:23). But later among the Cainites we have more extended (if perverted) versification:

> Adah and Zillah, hear my voice;
> Ye wives of Lamech, hearken unto my speech:
> For I have slain a man to my wounding,
> And a young man to my hurt.
> If Cain shall be avenged sevenfold,
> Truly, Lamech seventy and sevenfold! (Gen. 4:23-24).

The germ of mechanical industry is to be sought in the workshop of Tubal-Cain. Scripture specifically calls him a blacksmith,[21] and the Authorized or King James Version of the English Bible describes him as an "instructor of every artificer," that is, an entrepreneur or teacher of every manufacturer and engraver. Here then we also have the embryo of the fine arts as well as of heavy industry, as is evidenced by the name of Lamech's wife Adah—for "Adah"[22] means "adorn" or "ornaments." And as Tubal-Cain, the "instructor of every artificer" or engraver, was probably the manufacturer of this ornament with which Adah adorned herself, it is probable that the origin of all jewelry and sculpture and painting are to be found here too.

Now all of this quite considerable growth of culture among these godless Cainites was possible only because of the non-saving common grace which God so unmeritedly bestowed upon them in spite of their unbelief. For as Calvin remarked, together "with the evils which proceeded from the family of Cain, some good has been blended. For the invention of arts, and of other things which serve to the common use and convenience of life, is a *gift of God* by no means to be despised, and a faculty worthy of commendation. It is truly wonderful, that this race, which had most deeply fallen from integrity, should have excelled the rest of the posterity of Adam in rare endowments. I, however, understand Moses to have spoken

---

21. Gen. 4:22, Afrikaans Revised Version; cf. Hebrew *lōtēsh*, "a sharpener"; cf. AV, "instructor," and AV *margin*, "whetter."

22. Adah, cf. Gen. 4:19-23; cf. 4:22 AV, "artificer"; Hebrew *chorēsh*, "a plougher, engraver, manufacturer."

expressly concerning those arts, as having been invented in the family of Cain, for the purpose of showing that he was not so accursed by the Lord but that *He* would still scatter some excellent gifts among his posterity. . . . Moses, however, expressly celebrates the remaining benediction of God on that race, which otherwise would have been deemed void and barren of all good. Let us then know, that the sons of Cain, *though deprived of the Spirit of regeneration,* were yet endued with gifts of no despicable kind; just as the experience of all ages teaches us how widely the rays of divine light have shone on unbelieving nations, for the benefit of the present life; and we see, at the present time, that the *excellent gifts of the Spirit* are diffused through the *whole human race.* Moreover, the liberal arts and sciences have descended to us from the heathen. We are, indeed, compelled to acknowledge that we have received astronomy, and the other parts of philosophy, medicine, and the order of civil government, from them."[23]

Among the descendants of Cain in the city of Enoch, then, we find the beginnings of civilization. Here we specifically read of the birth of agriculture, of industry, and of music. The other descendants of Adam, such as Seth and his son Enos, developed liturgical culture and the cult of religion when they "began to call upon the name of the Lord" (Gen. 4:26), but it is among the sinful Cainites that culture reached its antediluvian peak, even though that culture became more and more degraded as the days of Noah approached.[24]

And it was precisely as a judgment against this degraded Cainite culture in the days of Noah that God sent the *diluvium* or great flood upon the earth!

*   *   *   *   *

Third, then, we must consider the impact of the Noachic covenant of general grace upon the further development of culture.

---

23. Calvin, *Commentary on Gen. 4:20;* cf. Lee, *Calvin on the Sciences* (London: Sovereign Grace Union, 1969), pp. 17-18.
24. Gen. 6:1-9; 8:21; Matt. 24:33f.; and especially Gen. 3 cf. II Thess. 2:7 and cf. Jansen van Rijssen, *Die Messias uit die Aarde* (Potchefstroom, South Africa: Pro Rege Press, 1956), pp. 19-31.

Noah was a great engineer, and it was this great cultural ability of his (perhaps at least in part learned from the Cainites?!) which enabled him to construct a seaworthy vessel large enough to save and to sustain his whole family as well as sufficient specimens of every single living land and air creature in the world inside that ark during the ravages of the great flood. And after the destruction of the city of Enoch and its evil inhabitants, when the flood waters had subsided from the face of the earth, God repeated His great cultural command to Noah and his family, whom God—doubtless after Noah had learned whatever was culturally useful from the doomed Cainites (wherewith he could later promote the arts anew)—had spared from the flood to continue with the immense task of subduing the earth. In this sense, Noah was a sort of "second Adam" (cf. Gen. 5:29). For, like the first Adam, Noah too was given the great cultural command to "be fruitful and multiply and replenish the earth"; and the beasts of the earth and the fowl of the air and the fishes of the sea were all delivered into the hand of Noah and of his sons (Gen. 6:1-7; cf. Ps. 8 and Heb. 2).

However, in order to permit culture to develop after the flood even more vigorously than previously, God now extended His common grace still further to mankind. Still further, for God had already manifested His common grace before the flood—namely by not executing the sentence of immediate physical death upon our first parents directly after the fall, as well as by protecting Cain from his enemies so that culture could develop among his descendants. But now, after the flood, God encouraged the development of culture still further, by extending His common grace to all mankind, in order to promote the general tranquillity of society—a condition indispensable to the development of culture, as we have seen above. Hence God (with His gift to all His earthly creatures of His breathtakingly beautiful rainbow) now guaranteed the regularity of climatic and seasonal changes (Gen. 8:22), guaranteed protection from wild animals by giving them the fear of mankind (Gen. 9:2, 3), and guaranteed law and order in human relationships by instituting law and political authority (including the death penalty!) as a means of curbing bloodshed (Gen. 9:5-6). This is therefore the germ of all government, the root of all law courts, judicial tribunals, prisons, congresses, senates, local municipalities, and administrations.

With regular rainfall and predictable seasons, with protection from wild beasts, and above all with the possibility of law and order in his own society, man could now set about his manifold tasks and the development of culture in relative peace. Hence we are told immediately of the development of grape-farming and viticulture in the sentence: "Noah began to be a husbandman, and planted a vineyard" (Gen. 9:20).

Clearly, all the preconditions had now been reached for the further extensive unfolding of human culture!

* * * * *

Fourth, it is necessary to consider next how the various national cultures of the world developed.

"Be fruitful and multiply, and replenish the earth!" Thus God commanded Adam before (Gen. 1:28) and Noah after (Gen. 9:1-7) the flood. But men were evil from their youth,[24] and they defied this commandment. They refused to fill the earth and to subdue it! They would not spread out and distribute and promote culture over the face of the earth! Like Cain, they decided to build a city—the earliest city of Babel or Babylon in the plain of Shinar in Mesopotamia (Gen. 10:8-12; 11:1-15). They had not learned the lesson of the flood. They refused to subdue the earth to the glory of God. Instead, they were bent on trying to subdue the glory of God and making a name for themselves!

The city of Babel and the tower of Babel which they built there, must indeed have been very imposing examples of early architecture, of ancient cultural achievement. But, paradoxical as it may seem, it was necessary for God to destroy this work of culture precisely in order to promote the tremendous works of culture over the whole earth which He had commanded men to do. For evil men had built this tower to keep themselves all together, "*lest* we be scattered abroad the face of the whole earth" (Gen. 11:4), so that they should not fill or "replenish the earth" and subdue it (Gen. 1:28), which God had created man *specifically* to *do!* (Acts 17:26). And it seems that their

33

urge to build the cosmopolitanizing and ecumenical tower was indeed prompted by a guilty anticipation of the judgment of God, on account of their refusal to spread culture over the whole earth, as well as by their desire to thwart the judgment of God. But the God of culture deliberately destroyed their tower, and He started to "confound their language, that they may not understand one another's speech"; and He "scattered them abroad the face of the earth" (Gen. 11:7-9).

Now this divine act of scattering mankind into the various nations throughout the world had at least two very important results. First, it resulted in man's filling the earth, replenishing it, and subduing it, or at least starting to do so in earnest, even as God had originally intended when He gave Adam the cultural command. And second, by channelizing the development of mankind into separate and different languages and nations, God laid the foundations for a vast enrichment of the world's cultures. Each nation would develop its own style of architecture, of philosophy, of poetry, etc. And—as ancient man spread out from Mesopotamia, into Greece and into Germany, or into Egypt and into Morocco, or into India and into Indonesia, or into China and into Japan, or across eastern Siberia and via western Alaska down into Mexico and Peru—art and music and folklore would all develop into a breathtakingly beautiful and almost endless variety of different cultural forms!

As a result of a variety of factors (such as the principle of pluriform personality, various and different divinely bestowed gifts, geographical isolation, the rigors of climate, natural resources, varying degrees of obedience and disobedience to the revealed will of God in nature, in history, and by contact with His covenant people of Israel), each nation also developed its own style of culture as a whole. Thus, Indian culture tended toward an intense mysticism which permeated all its music, philosophy, and religion. Nordic culture—the German in particular—tended toward an intense intellectualism, which left its mark on German philosophy and caused German scientists to achieve remarkable precision in the results of their research. The intense practicality of the Englishman—and even more so the American—has led to a remarkable productivity and to the development of commerce and expansion and technology at the

34

expense of philosophy and music. And the intense romanticism of the Irish has resulted in a wealth of folklore and poetry at the expense of economic development.

Other peoples remained relatively backward in their cultural development, notably the native inhabitants of Africa, Polynesia, and Australia. However, no matter how primitive a nation may seem to the outsider, each has its own God-given cultural treasures (*and* perverted cultural sins!) which distinguish it from its neighbor, for *"the most High* divided to the nations their *inheritance,* when He separated the sons of Adam" (Deut. 32:8). Yet it is only in orchestral union with all the other cultures of the world that the richness of each component culture playing its own predestinated part can truly be appreciated—even as it is only against the background of the basic unity of the Triune God (in Whose image cultural men are created) that the several various Persons of the most high Godhead can adequately be understood (Matt. 28:19; II Cor. 13:14).

It is quite impossible to trace the further spread of early culture in *all* its forms among all the nations in the world in a chapter of this brevity. It may, however, be helpful to make just a few observations about the development of culture in Israel in pre-exilic times.

*   *   *   *   *

Fifth, then, let us briefly consider the ancient Israelitic culture, which God used to preserve and to transmit His special revelation to all men everywhere thereafter.

Now it is true that the Israelitic culture, as opposed to all other cultures of the ancient world from about 2000 B.C. onward, was unique, in that it alone received sufficient special revelation from the Lord to develop an essentially theocratic culture, particularly as a result of the impact of the comprehensive Ten Commandments (Ex. 20; Deut. 5) on the whole of Israelitic life, as reflected in the concrete application thereof recorded in the specific political and social and ceremonial laws of Moses (Ex. 21–Deut. 30) and in the normative response of Israel thereto as recorded in the prophets (Isa.–Mal.). Much research still needs to be done in systematizing all this, and in extracting permanent cultural guidelines herefrom,

35

although (of course) guidelines which should be applied today only in the light of the later New Testament teachings.[25]

On the whole, however, as regards common revelation and common grace, just like the primitive and religious children of Seth before the flood, the children of Israel or the primitive and religious children of Abraham after the flood were considerably less culturally endowed than were their heathen neighbors. Indeed, we read of Moses that, "when he had come to years, [he] refused to be called the son of Pharaoh's daughter; choosing rather to suffer affliction with the children of God than to enjoy . . . the treasures of Egypt" (Heb. 11:25-26). The cultural treasures which the Israelites had formerly possessed and much of the knowledge previously brought by Abraham from Ur of the Chaldees near the site of the earliest city of Babylon (Gen. 11:9, 31), had, of course, been lost during the enslavement of the Israelites in Egypt, and so the cultural treasures which they possessed at the time of the exodus and thereafter (like the gold they took with them), were largely borrowed from the Egyptian civilization in the south, from the Babylonian culture in the east at the time of the exile, and from the Greeks in the west thereafter. The art of working with iron, for example, seems to have been derived from the Philistines (I Sam. 13:19-22). And even at the time of the climax of Israelitic civilization under David and Solomon, the foreign architect Hiram of Tyre in Phoenicia (I Kings 7:13-45) was commissioned to construct the brasswork of the temple in Jerusalem and all its accessories, even though that building was, of course, patterned after the God-designed tabernacle (Acts 7:44-47). Indeed, as the Lord Jesus Christ later remarked, "The children of this world are in their generation wiser than the children of light!" (Luke 16:8).

Yet Israelitic culture nevertheless steadily unfolded. Art among God's ancient people had reached a major peak in the work of Bezaleel and Aholiab in the manufacture of the tabernacle in the

---

25. In this regard, Koffieberg, *Het Mosaisch Recht en zijn Huidige Sociale Beteekenis,* and Smeenk, *Christelijk-Sociale Beginselen,* 2 vols. (Kampen: J. H. Kok, 1934), and Rushdoony, *The Institutes of Biblical Law* (Nutley, N. J.: The Craig Press, 1973), form useful introductory works.

wilderness, according to the exact blueprint specifications which God had shown Moses on Mount Sinai (Heb. 8:5). Of Bezaleel we are told that God "hath filled him with the Spirit of God, in wisdom, in understanding, and in knowledge, and in all manner of workmanship, and to devise curious works [that is, artistic ideas],[26] to work in gold, and in silver, and in brass, and in the cutting of stones to set them, and in the carving of wood. And He hath put in his heart that he may teach, both he and Aholiab, . . . them hath He filled with wisdom of heart, to work all manner of work: of the engraver, and of the cunning workman [that is, of the artist],[26] and of the embroider[er] in blue and purple, in scarlet and in fine linen, and of the weaver" (Ex. 35:30-35). But these artistic materials were largely fashioned from goods taken as spoils from Egypt (Ex. 12:35-36; 32:1-4; 35:5f., 22f.), just as the temple of Solomon was later constructed with wood obtained from the fir trees and cedars of Lebanon in Phoenicia (I Kings 5:8-10), and Solomon's palace (like King Jeroboam the Second's later mansion in Samaria?—Amos 6!) abounded with imported gold and silver and ivory and apes and peacocks (II Chron. 9:21). Indeed, it is even possible that Bezaleel and Aholiab may have achieved many of their artistic ideas from the Egyptians while in bondage, but, of course, expressed them in their own way under the guidance of Almighty God and to His glory as prescribed by the Lord God Himself (Ex. 24–27; 31:1-11).

Other aspects of Israelitic culture were perhaps more prominently developed. Music reached its finest expression in the use of the trumpet, the organ, and various types of percussion and stringed instruments such as the cymbals and the harp, in the temple liturgy (Ps. 150). Philosophy reached its climax where the Preacher, after searching unsuccessfully for the meaning of life in knowledge, in pleasure, in riches, and in fame, finally found it in the fear and service of God (Eccles. 1–6; 12). Poetry reached its summit in the Psalms and in the Song of Songs, as well as in the masterful description of the glories of God's creation in the closing chapters of the book of Job (chs. 38–41). While history is recorded with

---

26. Ex. 35:32, 35, Afrikaans Revised Version.

meticulous accuracy in the books of Kings and Chronicles, ending, as they do, with the sweeping away of culturally deteriorating Judah into the Babylonian captivity.

But even that catastrophe was by no means the end of the growth of godly culture! For God had pre-ordained even the exile and the subsequent developments to *enrich* His covenant people!

*   *   *   *   *

Sixth, then, let us lastly consider the growth of the old world cultures between the Old Testament and New Testament dispensations.

The famous existentialistic philosopher Karl Jaspers has pointed out that ancient thought peaked in the sixth century B.C. (namely, in the activities of Confucius and Lao-tse in China, of Vardhamana and Buddha in India, of Zoroaster and the Ishtar Gate in Mesopotamia, of the Ionians and the Eleatics among the Greeks, and of the Roman Republic in Italy. And from the Biblical perspective too, although the Egyptian and Assyrian cultures were now in decline, the prophecies of Daniel reveal that the "golden" or Chaldean culture of Nebuchadnezzar was then at its heyday[27] yet beginning to pass from the scene even as the "silver" or Medo-Persian culture of Cyrus was coming into ascendancy.[28] Later still, approximately a century after the Old Testament revelation closed at the time of the writing of the book of Malachi, the "brass" or Greek culture of Alexander the Great would overrun the other civilizations of the old world.[29] And lastly, less than a century before the commencement of the New Testament period, the mighty "iron" or Roman culture of the Caesars would carry all before it, Romanizing and amalgamating the remnants of the Near Eastern and the Hellenistic (and the neo-Egyptian) cultures in its wake."[30]

By the time of the birth of Christ, then, culture had spread throughout the ancient world. The art and architecture of Egypt and the science and philosophy of Greece had all passed their prime, and

---

27. Dan. 2:1, 31-32, 27-28; 7:1-4.
28. Dan. 2:32, 29; 7:5; 8:1-4, 20; 10:12-20.
29. Dan. 2:32, 39; 7:6; 8:5-8, 21-22; 10:20–11:4.
30. Dan. 2:33-35, 40; 7:7-9; 8:10-13; 9:26-27; 10:30-31; 12:1, 11 cf. **Matt.** 24:15-20, 28 and Luke 21:20-24.

38

either lingered on as a memory of a bygone and glorious past, or gradually declined into a ripe old age, or survived in a syncretized form, amalgamated together by the political genius of the Roman Empire, which was still playing its important role (Luke 23:38; John 19:19-22). Yet the real center of world history had now swung to Israel, the melting pot of Egyptian, Babylonian, and Grecian culture; to Israel, the land where the East meets the West; to Israel, the center of the earth. The wheel of history was turning, and Israel was the hub of that wheel, with Africa, Asia, and Europe as its spokes. Time reached its crossroads with the birth of Christ in Israel. Space reached its crossroads in Israel, the Middle East, the middle of the old world. World history had reached the crossroads in time and space. B.C. had met A.D. (Gal. 4:4), and East had met West (Isa. 43:5-6).

The growth of the culture of the ancient world had now been completed.

*　　*　　*　　*　　*

Let us summarize our findings of this chapter on the growth of culture in the world.

First of all, we saw that even non-Christian scholars agree that civilized cultures began to grow as from about 3000 B.C. onward, and that Mesopotamia seems to represent the cradle of civilization—as taught by the Bible too.

Second, it was seen that God Himself made it possible for man's culture to unfold, even after and in spite of the fall, by arresting the development of the full implications of sin by immediately promising that Jesus Christ as the Seed of the woman would later come to save elect man and all true culture and by having His Spirit strive with sinful man from immediately after the fall onward in order to guarantee the continuation of culture.

Third, it was shown that, between the fall and the flood, while cultic culture was developing among the Sethites, by God's common grace architecture and cattle ranching and music and weaving and poetry and metallurgy and industry strongly developed among the Cainites, in spite of their apostasy from the living God.

Fourth, we demonstrated that God's rainbow covenant with Noah

39

guaranteed all the essential prerequisites for the further development of culture, such as regular climatic and seasonal patterns, and protection from both wild animals and human criminals.

Fifth, it was seen that when the tower of Babel was built by sinful men precisely to attempt to thwart God's plan for the development of different cultures throughout the world, that God destroyed it, scattering different groups of men across the face of the earth, each group with its own language and each destined further to develop its own culture in its own characteristic way.

Sixth, we saw that the Old Testament Israelitic culture borrowed many cultural treasures from its Egyptian, Philistine, Phoenician, Babylonian, and Grecian neighbors, normatively reinterpreted them in terms of the Word of God, and thus used them to extend its own art and architecture and music and poetry and philosophy and history, generally to the glory of God—at least whenever obeying the leading of the Holy Spirit.

And seventh, we observed that the old world cultures peaked in the general time between the Old Testament and the New Testament dispensations, in which the amassed inheritances of the Egyptian, Babylonian, Persian, Greek, and Roman cultures all focused upon Israel.

* * * * *

What, then, can we learn from all this to benefit us today? In our present time of cultural flux, what guidelines can we derive from the ancient growth of culture?

First, as the Heidelberg Catechism suggests (Q. 9), we should observe that God not only does man no wrong in requiring him to execute the dominion charter even after the fall, but that He Himself actually promotes the development of human culture, even among the heathen, by His common grace, in spite of man's total depravity. For if, as the Westminster Confession says, even "the light of nature, and the works of creation and providence, do so far manifest the goodness, wisdom and power of God [that] there are some circumstances [even] concerning the worship of God and government of the Church, common to human actions and societies, which are to be ordered by the light of Christian prudence,"[31] how much more must this be the case[32] in the cultural life of the nations! For even "not elected" persons (and, surely, their cultures too!) "may have some common [grace] operations of the Spirit," which, while not saving them, do at least cause them to be "diligent to frame their lives according to the light of nature."[33]

Second, however, even though, as the Belgic Confession tells us, "the creation, preservation, and government of the universe . . . is before our eyes as a most elegant book, wherein all creatures, great and small, are as so many characters [or letters] leading us to see clearly the invisible things of God,"[34] we are nevertheless required to evaluate this whole world, including its sin-cursed heathen cultures, through what Calvin called the "spectacles of the Bible,"[35] whereby, the Belgic Confession goes on to tell us, God makes Himself even "more clearly and fully known."[34]

And third, we must appreciate that the God Who controls history from beginning to end, determined not to incarnate His Son until the old world civilizations had so unfolded that the necessary cultural climate for Christ's first coming had been created in the very "fullness of the time" (Gal. 4:4) and in the very center of the earth (Isa. 41:1, 5, 14). For the growth of the mighty cultures of Egypt and Babylon and Persia and Greece and Rome had all been predestinated by the sovereign Triune God to *serve*[36] the theocratic culture of Israel and to zero in on the advent of Christ in the very heart of the world.

* * * * *

For it is from Israel, the very center of the earth, that the God of

---

31. *Westminster Confession of Faith*, I:6.
32. *Ibid.*, I:1.
33. *Ibid.*, X:4.
34. *Belgic Confession*, art. 2.
35. Lee, *Philosophy and the Bible* (Cape May, N. J.: Shelton College Press, 1967), p. 1; cf. Calvin, *Institutes of the Christian Religion* (any ed.), I:6:1; I:13:3; I:14:1.
36. Cf. Wielenga, *op. cit.*, p. 265, "Egypt serves Israel. The Hellenistic culture yields material to the New Testament. Even modern cultures gives building materials to [the Christian] faith."

culture now commanded the nations of the world: "Look unto Me, and be ye saved, all the ends of the earth!" (Isa. 45:17, 22). For it was in *Israel* that all culture was now *to blossom* with the advent of the Second Adam Jesus Christ (I Cor. 15:45-47), Who came to redeem lost men and women—and to restore their culture too!

III

THE BLOSSOMING OF CULTURE

Any way we look at it, the advent of Jesus Christ as the rose of Sharon and the lily of the valley (Song 2:1) represents the very *blossoming* of the world's culture.

In the ancient Orient, Buddhism spoke of the jewel in the lotus flower,[1] but the modern Hindu Brahmo Samaj movement claims that Jesus is the only candidate in the field seriously bidding for the heart of the world.[2] The greatest Jewish philosopher of all time, Spinoza, asserted that, "It took Moses twenty-four hours to comprehend that which Jesus was able to grasp within one hour,"[3] while the great Jewish writer Sholem Asch has also shown a deep respect for Jesus,[4] and the great modern Jewish scholar Martin Buber has affectionately referred to Jesus as his elder brother. More significant still, even the fanatically anti-Christian modern Ahmaddiya sect of Islam has stated, "The Muslims are the true Christians, for they follow (or should follow) the true teaching of Christ. . . . Their real Muslim virtues (which from their point of view they call Christian virtues), entitle them to be called Christians, and to receive the leading position which (the anti-Islamic Christians) at present occupy in the world of men."[5]

---

1. Cf. Hess, *Siddharta: Eine Indische Dichtung* (New York Macmillan, 1962).
2. George, *The Unique Christ and the Mystic Gandhi* (Travancore, India: The Malabar Christian Office, 1934), p. 220.
3. Cf. Cahn, *The Philosophy of Judaism* (New York: Macmillan, 1962), p. 426.
4. Cf. especially Asch's trilogy, *The Nazarene, The Apostle,* and *Mary.*
5. Abdullah Yusif Ali, *The Holy Quran* (Lahore, Pakistan: Shaikh Muhammad (Ashraf Kashmiri Bazar, 1938), I, 137, n. 396.

Nor have modern evolutionists essentially differed. The historians Wallbank and Taylor inform us that "Christianity bears the unmistakable imprint of the personality of its founder, Jesus Christ," and that by the time of the Roman Emperor Nero's A.D. 65 persecutions, "Christian communities had already been established in all the important cities of the Roman empire."[6] The educationalists Rogers and Adams and Brown concede that Jesus' "ideals became a mighty force among the people of the Western world," and that today "There is hardly a country where Christian missionaries have not worked," Christianity itself representing "a great force in the struggle to civilize the world."[7]

Other evolutionists have also concurred: Darwin, it would appear, confessed Christ as his Savior before he died, describing the Bible as the only real book of any ultimate significance.[8] Thomas Huxley admitted that the Christian Scriptures are irreplaceable for the cultivation of true ethics.[9] And Fabian socialist H. G. Wells made the admission that Jesus Christ was quite foremost in the row of the world's great cultural figures.[10]

But perhaps the most remarkable testimony as to Christ's overtowering stature in the development of the cultural history of the world, comes from H. G. Wells's socialistic mentor, the renowned communist Karl Marx. For in his youth Marx insisted that, "The history of nations and the attitude of the individual proves the necessity of union with Christ. . . . Our heart, our understanding, history, the word of Christ, call out to us loudly and persuasively, that union with Him is an unconditional necessity, that we cannot reach our goal without Him."[11]

And if, as even *Marx* insists, neither we ourselves nor man's cul-

---

6. *Op. cit.*, pp. 197, 199.

7. *Op. cit.*, pp. 241, 243.

8. Cf. Enoch, *Evolution or Creation?* (London: Evangelical Press, 1968), pp. 166-167.

9. Thomas Huxley, *Contemporary Review*, December, 1870.

10. H. G. Wells, *American Magazine*, July, 1922.

11. Karl Marx, in Marx and Engels, *Werke, Ergänzungsband, I* (Berlin, East Germany: Dietz Verlag—Institüt für Marxismus-Lenismus der SED, 1964–1968), I, 598-601.

ture can bloom without union with Christ—who are we Christians (in *this* matter!) to disagree? For as regards the world's great cultural leaders, Jesus Christ is indeed "the chiefest among ten thousand!" (Song 5:10).

* * * * *

In this chapter, on the blossoming of culture, then, we shall successively discuss: first, the crisis of world culture at the birth of Jesus Christ; second, the blossoming of man's culture in the earthly life of Jesus; third, the cultural significance of the resurrection and ascension and heavenly session of our Lord; fourth, the renewal of culture through the operation of the outpoured Spirit; fifth, the struggle for cultural balance among Christians before the Protestant Reformation; and sixth, the triumph of Christian culture among Christians at the time of the Reformation and thereafter.

* * * * *

First, then, let us look at the cultural crisis of the world at the time of Christ's incarnation.

The mighty Roman Empire had spread across the face of the old world. It had indeed brought a great measure of political stability to the warring little nations it had swallowed up. But in the wake of their lost freedom, the various conquered peoples of the empire sank into the despair of defeat. Their tribal gods had failed to protect them; their old, familiar order had passed away; there was little hope for the future. The peoples began to live in a spiritual vacuum. In their crisis of existence, they began to seek anew for the meaning of life.[12] And the Lord God of culture was not to disappoint them! For soon the eyes of all the elect were to be focused on the blossoming of all culture—on the incarnation of the Lord of culture Himself in the land of Israel (I Tim. 3:16). For Christ alone could give those dying cultures a new lease of life, and He did so "when the fulness of time was come, when God sent forth His Son, made of a woman, made under the law, to redeem them that were under the law, [so] that we might receive the adoption of sons [of God]!" (Gal. 4:4-5).

12. Cf. Groenewald, *Handboek Bybelse Geskiedenis: Die Nuwe Testament* (Pretoria, South Africa: Interkerklike Uitgewerstrust, 1968), pp. 27-56.

45

"And it came to pass in those days, that there went out a decree from Caesar Augustus, that all the world should be taxed. . . . And Joseph went up from Galilee . . . unto the city of David, which is called Bethlèhem . . . to be taxed with Mary, his espoused wife, being great with child. . . . And she brought forth her first-born son" (Luke 2:1-7), "and His Name was called Jesus" (Luke 2:21).

With the birth of Jesus Christ, God gave the world *His greatest cultural treasure*.[13] And the elect of all the nations had waited for Him! (Isa. 25:9). From the East, wise men responded and gave Him their treasures: gold, and frankincense and myrrh (Matt. 2: 1, 11). From the West, King Herod, the representative of the Roman Empire, realized that a new King had entered history (Matt. 2:31-32). God had prepared His Son, His greatest treasure, "before the face of all the people—a light to lighten the Gentiles and the glory of His people Israel" (Luke 2:31-32). The "Desire of all nations" had come! (Hag. 2:7).

And Who is this "Desire of all nations," this Savior of the world, Jesus Christ? Before His birth as man, He had existed from all eternity as God the Son, alongside of God the Father and God the Holy Spirit.[14] He is the eternal Word of God, Who was in the beginning with God, and Who is Himself God (John 1:1, 14). He is Himself the Maker of all things, for by Him all things were made (John 1:1, 3)—*all* things: art and music, science and philosophy, law and poetry—all culture! He is the Wisdom of God (Prov. 8: 12-31; I Cor. 1:24, 30), the Beginning of all philosophy and science (Col. 2:2-9); He is the Word of God,[15] the Beginning of all literature and poetry. He is the Artist of creation,[16] Who rejoiced before His Father in the work of His hands, and in man, His masterpiece, His

---

13. John 3:16 cf. Col. 1:13-17; 2:2-3.
14. Gen. 1:1-3; John 1:1, 14; 17:1-5; Heb. 9:14.
15. John 1:1, 4, 9, 14 cf. Eph. 3:14-15; Gen. 1:3, 26.
16. Prov. 8:30 cf. American Standard Version and A.B.V.A. or the Afrikaans Bible with Explanatory Notes (Cape Town, South Africa: United Protestant Publishers, 1959), II, 1356, which comments here: "If we vocalize [the Hebrew word] as 'ommanu,' we can translate it as 'artist,' cf. Song 7:2 and the Assyrian word 'ummanu,' which means 'architect.' "

own workmanship, His poem,[17] His own image. And when this only begotten Son of God Who was in the very bosom of the Father became flesh in Christ Jesus, He *declared* the God of culture (John 1:18). For the God of culture declared His fullness by pouring out all His own cultural fullness into Jesus Christ, "in Whom are hid[den] all the treasures of wisdom and knowledge" (Col. 2:2-3), "in Whom dwelleth all the fullness of the Godhead bodily" (Col. 2:9), and on Whom the Spirit of the Lord rested, "the Spirit of wisdom and understanding, the Spirit of counsel and . . . knowledge" (Isa. 11:2).

And with Christ's incarnation, the beginning of the end of the world's cultural crisis was now in sight!

* * * * *

Second, let us look at the blossoming of man's culture in the earthly life of Jesus Christ the Second Adam. For it was this same God the Son Who had created the first Adam (John 1:1-3)—and Who had given him the great cultural command to subdue the world (Gen. 1:28)—Who Himself became the Second Adam and *really* did this! (I Cor. 15:22, 45-47). For just as the Triune God, while continuing with His work of maintaining the universe, commenced His seventh day (co-extensive with world history) in order *to make* the universe (Gen. 2:3, *margin*) through the efforts of the first Adam and his descendants—so too did Jesus as the Second Adam during His earthly life work concurrently with the Triune God, saying, "My Father worketh hitherto [or, up to now], and I work [too]!" (John 5:17).

This same God the Son, we say, incarnated Himself as the Second Adam[18] and had dominion over the earth and the sea and the sky. It was this same God the Son Who had given "Solomon wisdom and understanding exceeding much, . . . and Solomon's wisdom excelled the wisdom of all the children of the earth . . . and all the wisdom of Egypt"; wisdom to help execute the dominion charter over the fish of the sea and over the fowl of the air and over all the beasts and over all the earth and over every creeping thing that creepeth upon

---

17. Eph. 2:10, Greek *poema*, "a poem, a work"; cf. AV, "workmanship"; cf. Eph. 4:24 and John 1:15.
18. Rom. 5:12f. cf. I Tim. 3:16 cf. I Cor. 15:22, 45-47 cf. Matt. 12:42.

the earth (Gen. 1:26), for Solomon "spake three thousand proverbs: and his songs were a thousand and five. And he spake of trees, from the cedar tree that is in Lebanon even unto the hyssop that springeth out of the wall: he spake also of beasts, and of fowl, and of creeping things, and of fishes" (II Kings. 4:29-34). And it was this same God the Son Who, during His own earthly life, discoursed about the lilies of the field and the fowl of the air and the beasts of the field and the fishes of the sea with far greater wisdom than even Solomon ever did.[19] For it was this same Son of God Who was incarnated both as the Second Adam and as the Greater Solomon[18] and Who— anointed with the all-enabling Spirit *without measure* (John 3:34)— kept the Adamitic covenant which the first Adam transgressed and Who executed the cultural commandment which the first Adam had failed to carry out. For Jesus Christ subdued the earth, and had dominion over the sea and the air and the land and all their inhabitants.

The Second Adam exercised His dominion over the sea. He could walk on the surface of the sea at will (Mark 6:45f.), whereas His disciples needed a boat. He could calm the raging tempest and subdue the waves by the naked power of His authoritative command, whereas His followers would have drowned had He not done so (Matt. 8:23f.). He could instantly summon an abundance of fish into the nets of His disciples, after they had toiled all night and caught nothing (John 21:3-11). "Behold, what manner of man is this, that even the winds and the sea obey Him!" (Matt. 8:27).

But Christ the Second Adam also dominated the land. He conquered the wilderness and moved unharmed among the wild beasts of the earth (Mark 1:13). He cursed the fig tree, and it wilted under His command (Matt. 21:18f.). He utilized the wood of trees—as the Master Carpenter (6:3). And He raised the dead from their earthly tombs to the wonderment of the onlookers (John 11:38f.).

And Christ the Second Adam also subdued the air and the sky. At His birth, a multitude of the heavenly host gave glory to God in the highest (Luke 2:13-15). At His death, the very sun was extinguished, to acknowledge the extinguishing of a Greater Light.[20]

19. Cf. Matt. 6:26f.; 7:6f.; 12:42 and 13:47f.
20. Matt. 27:45 cf. Mal. 4:2 and John 8:12.

And at His ascension, He was carried up into heaven, and a cloud received Him out of sight (Luke 24:51; Acts 1:9).

So Jesus Christ, the Second Adam, subdued the earth and all its fullness. With contempt did He reject the devil's offer to give Him all the kingdoms of the world and all the glory of them (Matt. 4: 8-10)—for these kingdoms had belonged to Jesus all the time! They were His by creation! And, after His execution of the Adamitic covenant on Calvary's tree where He bled and died to save the elect from the wrath of God for their transgressing the Adamitic covenant (Hos. 6:7, margin), all these kingdoms of the world—represented in the Hebrew and Greek and Roman languages nailed to His cross (Luke 23:38; John 19:19-22)—became His by redemption too! (Rev. 11:15). For as the Heidelberg Catechism so correctly informs us, our divine Savior became *the Second* Adam, so that "He might bear *in His human nature* the burden of God's wrath, and that He might *obtain for us* and *restore to us,* righteousness and life!" (Q. & A. 17).

Thus did culture blossom in the earthly life of of Jesus. And that flowering was "altogether lovely!" (Song 5:16).

*   *   *   *   *

Third, we must next consider the cultural significance of the resurrection, ascension, and heavenly session of Jesus.

After His successful execution of the Adamitic covenant perfected on Calvary's cross through the shedding of the blood of the everlasting covenant in order to save and to sanctify His children (Heb. 13:20; Matt. 26:28), the risen Christ as the triumphant Second Adam in all His glorified beauty (Dan. 10:3-6; Rev. 1:13-20) ordered His followers, His descendants, to execute the covenant further. His descendants. For He bore them in His wounds, brought them forth from His bleeding body in their moment of birth and His moment of death. In that moment, "He saw His seed," He foresaw all His children. He saw all the travail, the birth-pangs of His soul, and brought about the birth, the rebirth, of His descendants—Who were born from above, born of God, born in and from the human body assumed by God the Son (Isa. 53:10-11; John 1:12-13; 3: 3-13). And as the Second Adam, the resurrected Christ commands

49

His regenerated descendants: "Go . . . and teach all nations, baptizing them, . . . teaching them *all things whatsoever* I have commanded you" (Matt. 28:19-20)—*including* the cultural things I commanded you to do which I, the Word of God, previously commanded Adam to do (John 1:1-5; Gen 1:1-3, 26-28). "Go ye into all the world!" (Mark 16:15). And in so saying, Christ in effect repeats and expands what He had previously said to the first Adam and his descendants: "Replenish the earth!" (Gen. 1:28).

Go ye into all the world and . . . subdue the earth!

Through the resurrection of Christ the Second Adam from the dead, we too are resurrected from the death of sin and recreated in the image of God unto new life—that is, unto new *cultural* life to the glory of the Lord. "For if we be dead [unto sin] with Christ, we believe that we shall also live with Him. Knowing that Christ being raised from the dead dieth no more; death hath no more dominion over Him" (Rom. 6:8-9). Neither, the apostle goes on to say, has sin dominion over those who are in Christ (Rom. 6:14), for those who are in Christ have dominion over sin (cf. Gen. 4:7), yea, dominion over the whole earth and the whole sea and the whole sky (Gen. 9:1-7; I Cor. 3:21-23)—inasmuch as they have put off the old man and put on the new man which is renewed in knowledge after the image of Him that created him! (Col. 3:9-10; Gen 1:28).

In Christ's ascension into heaven, Christians and their culture are even more exalted than they were by Christ's resurrection from the dead. For when Jesus went back to heaven, the Son of man as "God went up with a shout," to become "a great King over all the earth," and "to subdue the people under us, and the nations under our feet" (Ps. 47:7, 2-3). "Thou hast ascended on high, Thou hast led captivity captive: Thou hast received gifts for men; yea, for the rebellious also, that the Lord God might dwell among them" (Ps. 68:18). For "He that ascended, ascended up far above all things, that He might fill all things" (Eph. 4:9-10). And we who are His workmanship, *created in Christ Jesus unto good works,* have already in spirit been raised from the dead and made to sit together in heavenly places in Christ Jesus! (Eph. 2:10, 6).

In Christ's heavenly session, God gathered *all* things together in

50

heaven and on earth (including man's cultures!), and appointed Christ to sit "at His own right hand in heavenly places far above all principality, and power, and might, and dominion, and every name that is named, not only in this world, but also in that which is to come: and hath put all things under His feet, and gave Him to be the Head *over all things* to the Church, which is His body, the fulness of Him that filleth all in all!" (Eph. 1:10, 20-23). God hath put *all* things without exception under Christ's feet, although "we see *not yet* all things put under Him. But we see Jesus," and *now* the Son of man is already reigning, seated on His heavenly throne (Heb. 2: 8-9). "For He must reign, *till He hath put all enemies under His feet,*" when "cometh the end, when He shall have delivered up the Kingdom to God, even the Father; when He shall have put down all rule and all authority and power" (I Cor. 15:25, 24).

What a tremendous comfort, even as regards the future development of human culture here on earth, to know that the resurrected and ascended and heavenly enthroned Second Adam—and *we* in Him—now rules the universe as man, ever subduing it and bringing it more and more under His control in practice too through the Christ-directed expansion of His Spirit-filled earthly Church!

* * * * *

Fourth, then, the enthroned Christ even *renews* man's culture through His outpoured Spirit. For after elect men and their culture were redeemed on Calvary and vindicated on Easter Sunday and spiritually uplifted in Christ's ascension and overruled forever from His heavenly session onward, elect men and their culture were *renewed* and energized on the day of Pentecost with dynamic power by the enthroned Christ from on high in the Person of God's mighty Spirit not many days after Christ's ascension and heavenly session.

Pentecost indeed in principle cancelled the disruptive effects which the destruction of the tower of Babel had brought down on man and his culture, but it did not cancel the principle of pluriformity as such. To the contrary, at Pentecost "every nation under heaven" heard in its own "tongue[s] the wonderful works of God" (Acts 2:5, 11). And in the renewing work of the outpoured Spirit of God, in the comprehensive cosmic signs of wind and fire and smoke

51

and darkness and rain and blood (Acts 2:1-20), we are presented with a total view of the recreation of created reality, namely the renewal of the metaphysical universe and of man and all his culture as a part thereof.

Thenceforth the Creator Spirit would not destroy His pluriform creation and renewed man as the crown thereof. The early Christians worked together as a real community, but this community in no way overshadowed the individuality of its members nor their individual cultural insights.[21] Thus, each regenerated separate national and personal cultural insight into created and recreated reality is preserved, sanctified, and expanded. The national cultural insights of the Athenians (Acts 17:23, 28) and of the Cretans (Tit. 1:12-13), for example, are preserved and sanctified and expanded, as too are the different personalities of the apostles Peter and Paul and John.[22] The Spirit of the Lord cleanses not only our hearts and our bodies but also our intellects and hence our cultural insights too, for He is "the Spirit of wisdom and understanding, the Spirit of counsel and might, the Spirit of knowledge and of the fear of the Lord"; and when "the Spirit of the Lord shall rest upon him"—upon him who is sanctified by the Spirit (that is, primarily the Lord Jesus, but, by implication, also the children of God who possess the same Spirit, albeit in lesser and qualitatively different measure)—the Spirit "shall make him of quick understanding in the fear of the Lord" (Isa. 11:2-3).

Hence, the Spirit-filled Christian too is to be equipped with God-given wisdom, understanding, counsel, knowledge, and (above all) the fear of the Lord—even in (or rather especially in) his cultural activity. For as the Heidelberg Catechism tells us (Q. 32), I am called a Christian precisely because "I am a member of Christ by faith and thus a partaker of His [Holy Spirit] anointing [cf. John 3:34; Acts 2:17; I John 2:27], that I may confess His Name

---

21. Acts 2:42-47; 4:32-37; 5:1-4; 6:1-5; I Thess. 4:4-12; II Thess. 3:6-15; I Cor. 12:1-30; Eph. 4:4-16; 6:1-9; and cf. Lee, *Onheilige Dialoog tussen Katolisisme en Kommunisme,* in *Antikom-Nuusbrief* (Pretoria, South Africa: April, 1970).

22. Cf. Acts. 15:7-22; Gal. 2:7-16; II Pet. 1, 13-18; 3:15-16; Rev. 1:9; 21:2; 22:8.

[and] present myself a living sacrifice of thankfulness to Him!"

Moreover, as we have seen, Christ as the Second Adam was engaged in the works of subduing the earth and the sea and the sky. And as He Himself declared: "He that believeth on Me, the works that I do shall he do also; and *greater* works than these shall he do; *because* I go unto My Father" (John 14:12)—because Christ would thereafter send His Spirit down into His Church to impel her to undertake these even greater works for Christ's sake! And each Christian mentioned in the New Testament did this in his or her own way. Dorcas made coats and garments for the poor; Cornelius was a faithful army officer; Rhoda was a housemaid for Mary the mother of John Mark; Paul not only preached but also made tents; Sergius governed the island of Cyprus; Lydia was a businesswoman; the Philippian kept a jail; Apollos was an orator; Erastus was a chamberlain or the treasurer of a city; Luke was a beloved physician; and Zenas was a lawyer—all and only to the glory of God! (Acts 8:36, 39; 10:1-2, 22; 12:12-15; 13:7-12; 16:14, 36; 18:24; Rom. 16:23; I Cor. 10:31; Col. 4:14; Tit. 3:13).

We are not for one moment suggesting that Christ came to earth *only to* subdue the earth and the sea and the sky. To the contrary, the primary reason for His incarnation and atonement was to save sinners and to make His children partakers of the divine nature by His divine power (I Tim. 1:15; II Pet. 1:3-4). For Christ is *far more* than just the Second Adam. Indeed, "the first man is of the earth, earthy: the Second man is the Lord from heaven. . . . And as we have borne the image of the earthy, we shall also bear the image of the Heavenly [man]" (Cor. 15:47, 49). Yet inasmuch as Christ is *also* the Second *Adam* (I Cor. 15:22, 45) and according to His humanity a Descendant of the first Adam (Luke 3:23, 38), we Christ-ians, as "descendants" of both Adams (Rom. 5:12f.; Isa. 53:10), are to promote *both* the dominion charter of the first Adam and the great commission of the Second Adam as but two aspects of *one* harmonious Christ-ian or (Second) Adam-ic mandate! (Heb. 2:3-16; 4:3-4, 11, 14-16).

So now, Christians, by the power of the indwelling Spirit of Christ, must go forth with the Gospel in *all* its fullness, preaching salvation

53

to the whole man (Rom. 10:9), and subduing the entire earth (Acts 1:5-8). Through them, the covenant-keeping descendants of the Second Adam, "God would make known among the Gentiles [or the heathen nations], what is the riches of the glory of this mystery, which is: 'Christ in you,' the Hope of glory!" (Col. 1:26-28). And Christ must be preached by Christians, "teaching every man in all wisdom" and "striving according to His working" (Col. 1:28-29). For Christians must warn every man that Christ the only Savior of hell-deserving sinners (Acts 4:12; 16:31), is also the God of culture, the Wisdom of God, the Second Adam, the Lord of glory! (I Cor. 2:8).

Christ must be *preached!* Yet Christians dare not confine their preaching only to the salvation of the souls of man—*vitally* important as that unquestionably is! For Christ saves not merely the *soul* of man; He save the *whole* man—soul *and* body *and* mind! Nor can Christians even be satisfied with merely *preaching* all the counsel of God (Acts 20:27). In addition, they must also *practice* what they preach! (James 1:25-27). Again, Christ is not just the Savior of *man*—He is also the Savior of the *world,* and all its fullness. He is not only the human Christ—He is not merely the cosmic Christ— He is also the Divine Christ, God the Son, the Lord of all the *universe!*

Lord of *all* the universe! *This* must be the scope of the Christian's testimony in the world of culture! Not merely *"youth* for Christ," but also *"art* for Christ," *"politics* for Christ," *"philosophy* for Christ," *"science* for Christ," *"culture* for Christ," yes, *everything* for Christ! The culturally minded Christian is called by God to develop a Christian art and a Christian literature, a Christian philosophy and a Christian educational system, Christian business methods and Christian relaxations—yea, in fact, a Christian *culture!* The Christian who *confines* his religion to soul-winning and church attendance— *vital* as these are—is, in fact, confining the full scope of the blood of the cross, which was shed to reconcile *all* things, "whether they be things in earth, or things in heaven" (Col. 1:20). For, "at the Name of Jesus, every knee should bow, of things in heaven, and things on earth, and things under the earth. And every tongue should confess that Jesus Christ is Lord, to the glory of God the Father" (Phil. 2:10-11).

So therefore, in the power of the indwelling Spirit—"whether therefore ye eat, or drink, or *whatsoever* ye do, do *all* to the glory of God!" (I Cor. 10:31)

* * * * *

Fifth, we must note the struggle for cultural balance among Christians before the time of the Protestant Reformation.

It is true that the tiny Christian Church in its first period, although limited in its influence on the broad course of cultural events in the Roman world, did recognize that government and science and art and music and philosophy and architecture were divine institutions and gifts from God, as Bavinck points out in his *Calvin and Common Grace*.

It should not be thought, however, that the clear teaching of the Old Testament that man must glorify God in the totality of his entire *earthly* existence and the clear teaching of the New Testament that the risen and ascended Christ is to be recognized as Lord over *every* area of human life, was *heeded* by *all* the early Christians, any more than it is heeded by all Christians today. In point of fact, even during apostolic times, many Christians had an incorrect vision of the nature of Christ's Kingdom.

For example, some of the early Hebrew Christians thought that Christ had come to establish merely a political kingdom for the Jews only, who were to be liberated from Roman domination in the land of Palestine alone (John 6:15; Acts 1:6). Whereas in actual fact, Jesus had come to establish a Kingdom in and over every nation (John 18:36-37; Rev. 11:15), a Kingdom destined to expand triumphantly throughout the whole earth (Matt. 28:18-20; Ps. 22:27-31; and Rom. 4:17).

At the opposite pole, some of the early Thessalonian Christians seem to have thought that Christ's Kingdom had not yet been established in this world here and now, but would commence only after Christ's second coming (I Thess. 4:14-18; cf. II Thess. 1 and 2). Whereas in actual fact, Christ translates His children into the

Kingdom of God right here on earth at the very time of their regeneration (Col. 1:13; John 3:3-5).

Then again, there was also the Corinthian heresy, where some of the Christians in that congregation had tended to restrict the presence of God's Kingdom to church life alone (and a very narrow and local concept of the Church at that—I Cor. 1:11-15; 14:23f.), and in practice to deny the kingship of Christ over the extra-ecclesiastical areas of life, such as juridical litigation (I Cor. 6), marriage (I Cor. 7), and social affairs (I Cor. 8), in which they were still thoroughly conformed to the spirit of the world rather than to the spirit of Christianity (cf. Rom. 11:36–12:2). In actual fact, however, Christ's Kingdom embraces every area of life (Ps. 103:19; Col. 1:13-20).

This struggle for cultural balance in the lives of God's people did not terminate during the apostolic era but continued even among post-apostolic Christians, as typically seen in the vastly differing cultural outlooks of Clement, of Tertullian, and of Augustine.

Titius Flavius Clemens or Clement of Alexandria and his even greater pupil Origen both demonstrated the great danger of a syncretistic attitude to culture "not after Christ" (cf. Col. 2:8), by seeking to combine Christianity with non-Christian cultural views and attitudes. Converted to Christianity only after imbibing much Greek and Oriental culture and Gnosticism, Clement (A.D. 150–216) attempted to synthesize especially Greek culture with the Biblical life and world view (cf. Philo). Consequently, he erroneously regarded Christianity as basically a system of philosophy and a means of deifying man, to which Christian system one can graduate from Greek thought (where the Son of God and the divine Logos had, he believed, even enlightened Plato, the greatest of all philosophers). To Clement, man had two souls, a carnal or secular one and a rational or sacred one; the sex act, essentially evil, caused the fall; man is now not totally depraved, but still has a free will; and a future purgatory will ultimately cleanse the wicked. And his pupil Origen even went on to claim the equal duration of creation alongside of God even from eternity past (cf. Aristotle), and the infinite successive "creation" of different worlds and man's ultimate union with God (cf. Hinduism)!

56

Truly, such a wholesale and unscriptural absorption of non-Christian cultural elements into Christianity is essentially destructive of Christianity as such.

The opposite error, however, namely that of trying to avoid all cultural involvement whatsoever, is to be found in Tertullian of Carthage (A.D. 160–230). Tertullian, previously a lawyer, and converted to Christianity at the age of forty, was so violently opposed to non-Christian Gnostic philosophy, that he over-reacted thereagainst. Confining his Christianity to church activities alone, he not only became extremely ascetic but also started attacking other Christians who held political office under the Roman emperors. He also condemned Christian artists and even military service and second marriages. Not surprisingly, he ultimately quit the orthodox branch of the Church and joined a proto-Pentecostalistic-type spiritualistic sect known as the Montanists, where he fulminated against the Roman and Greek cultures to his heart's content.

Truly, such a wholesale repudiation of the cultural insights God has given people outside of church life is also essentially destructive of Christianity, because it not only tends to make such Christians so heavenly minded that they become no earthly use, but worse still because it also sometimes makes them spiritually proud and haughty—for (so *they* think!) *they* are not like the wretched unbelievers, and *they* have no use for all that "worldly" culture!

The third typical position of the early Church—and the essentially correct one—was that of Augustine of Hippo. Born in Carthage in A.D. 354, he received a thorough education in the Latin and Greek classics, and then sought rest for his passionate soul first in Manichaeanism and then in neo-Platonism (and especially in that of Plotinus). But his soul found no rest until it later came to rest in Christ, as a result of hearing the preaching of Ambrose of Milan, after which he developed the greatest system of essentially orthodox Christian thought that the world was to see for the next thousand years.

Augustine wrote fifteen volumes on the Trinity, asserting that God is the highest truth, good, and beauty, the Ground of all being and form, essentially distinct from all other (created) being. Cosmogonically, this present creation is the only creation, exnihilated with and in time, to the glory of God. Cosmologically, all that God created is "very good" and triunely reflects His Trinity, and is sustained in its dependent being by God's continual providence—matter is *good!*

As regards man, Augustine denied the preexistence of the soul (as then asserted by non-Christian culture), while regarding it as the highest of all creatures and as triune (memory, understanding, and will); it thus reflects the Trinity. However, the body is in no sense the prison of the soul (*per contra,* Plato). Man was created according to the image of God; all the aspects of man are completely harmoniously related to one another; and Adam was possessed of great intuitive wisdom, was not subject to laborious exhaustion, and was lord of the animals, etc.

As regards original sin, it had cosmic proportions, damned the entire human race in Adam's historic transgression, whence it is transmitted to every one of his descendants by natural generation. Accordingly, it was now necessary, after being saved by the blood of Christ, to believe the Holy Scriptures in order to arrive at further truth, so that all science and culture should be Christian.

Culturally, the entire course of world history represents the unfolding of the mighty struggle between the forces of good and the forces of evil, in every area of human activity, between the City of God and the City of Babylon. Moreover, this struggle is predestined ultimately to result in the decisive and permanent triumph of the City of God in every sphere of man's endeavors.

All this is *not* to say that Augustine's view of culture was *100%* Biblical! Quite frankly, it was not, for he still tended to elevate the soul above the body, the Church above the state, faith above reason, the so-called clergy above the so-called laymen, theology above philosophy, and ecclesiastical matters above cultural pursuits. Yet notwithstanding all this, Augustine's cultural outlook was still basically molded according to the triune Biblical cultural motive of creation-redemption-consummation (Rom. 11:36).

In the late Middle Ages, the great Thomas Aquinas minimized the strengths of Augustine's position and enlarged Augustine's weaknesses in Thomas's own attempts to find a common basis of cultural contact between Christianity and the world of non-Christian culture. Acutely aware of what he regarded as the need to find a widely acceptable basis for cultural liaison between (Platonistic or Aristotelian) Jews and Moslems and Christians, Aquinas relegated all cultural areas outside of the Church and theology to the so-called "secular realm," where reason (which he believed is qualitatively the same among Jews and Moslems and Christians) was to reign, while elevating the Church and theology to the level of the so-called "sacred realm," where faith (which he believed is possessed by Christians alone) was to reign.

The importance of Thomas Aquinas in the history of the development of culture can hardly be overestimated. As Buswell maintains, his "schizocosmic"[23] division of reality into the "sacred" and the "secular" realms in principle separated the Bible from science and Christianity from culture, and this tendency still lives on today not only in Roman Catholicism and semi-Reformed pietism, but also (and, of course, even more radically!) in Western humanism. In actual fact, however, there are *not* two realms, a sacred and a secular, at all! There is only *one* kind of *realm,* namely, *Christ's Kingdom over God's universe,* ruled over by *King Jesus,* where *everything* is essentially *sacred* because Christ's Kingdom *ruleth over all!* (Ps. 103:19). Before sin, there was no tension at all between nature and grace, for God was "gracious" in giving man the use of "nature," and at that time nature was always a channel of "grace" (*alias* God's unmerited favor). For after creation and before the fall, "God saw *every thing* that He had made, and behold, it was *very* good" (Gen. 1:31). And, even though sin subsequently stained all things in the universe (Rom. 8:19-22), nevertheless, as a result of the cosmos-embracing work of Christ whereby He reconciled *all* things in earth and in heaven (Col. 1:20), today too *"every* creature of God is good, and *nothing* is to be refused, *if* it be received with thanksgiving: for it is sanctified by the Word of God and prayer" (I Tim. 4:4-5).

There are *not,* then, two different realms, a sacred and a secu-

---

23. Buswell, *Thomas and Bible* (Ringwood, N. J.: Shelton College Press, n.d.); cf. too his *The Philosophies of F. R. Tennant and John Dewey* (New York: Philosophical Library, 1950).

lar. There *are*, however, two different kinds of *people* living in God's one realm or rather laboring in God's one workshop: namely, *non-Christian* people with their secular evaluation of the whole of life, and *Christian* people with their sacred evaluation of the whole of life—including culture. Christians, of course, can be—and too often are!—affected by worldly attitudes toward some or all aspects of God's universe, which worldly attitudes they derive partly from their "old man" or their remaining evil nature (Eph. 2:1-3; 4:17-22), and partly from their continuing contact with worldly non-Christians (John 17:6-16; I John 2:15-17), and, sadly, even with worldly Christians (I Cor. 6). The true Christian's mandate from God, however, is clear: Be not conformed to this world, but be transformed by the renewing [or regeneration] of the mind, so that *the whole man* be presented or dedicated as a living sacrifice unto God, from Whom and through Whom and to Whom are *all* things, including the things of *culture*—which dedication, after all, is but our reasonable divine service and our required religious devotion unto the Lord! (Rom. 11:36-12:2).

After the perverted development of Christian attitudes toward culture from Clement and Tertullian through Thomas Aquinas,[24] the people of God were now ripe for further reformation!

* * * * *

Lastly, then, let us examine the triumph of Christian culture among Christians at the time of the Protestant Reformation and thereafter.

After the time of Thomas Aquinas, the Romish Church (by more and more elevating the importance of the Church work of the clergy above the so-called "secular work" of the so-called "laymen") so dominated all expression of authentic Christianity and so extended its own control over the whole of man's culture, that even the Church itself became strongly conformed to the spirit of the world (Rom. 12:2). This had happened because, it will be remembered, the highly influential Aquinas had *in principle* declined to Christianize the so-called "secular areas" of life, which secularism now pro-

---

24. Cf. Lee, *A Christian Introduction to the History of Philosophy* (Nutley, N.J.: The Craig Press, 1969), pp. 109-111, 115-117, 132-137, 225-226.

ceeded to poison the Church once the Church had swallowed them up in their unchristianized or rather dechristianized form! The *De*formed Church, conformed to the spirit of the world, desperately needed to become the *Re*formed Church, transformed by the renewing work of the Holy Ghost!

As a result of the deformation of the Church, wildcat sects of revolutionary social drop-outs known as the Anabaptists (*not* to be confused with our modern Baptist brethren!) opposed the entire "establishment"—Church and state, economics and art, science and literature. To the Anabaptistic mentality (compare that of the modern hippies and yippies), culture was *essentially* evil, and the true Christian was to be essentially anti-cultural.

Fortunately, however, the already Deformed Church was spared such further deformation to any significant extent at the hands of the Anabaptists. For, under the godly and eminently sane leadership of Martin Luther and John Calvin, the Deformed Church was now at least in part turned into the Reformed Church.

Luther opposed both Rome and the Anabaptists, and helped restore a cultural balance not only in his down-to-earth *Table Talks* but also by insisting on the dignity of everyday labor as a *Beruf* or godly calling even for or rather *especially* for the saved Christian. Before the Reformation, Rome had taken the position that the only truly divine calling was that of a monk; Luther, however, insisted that monks had *no* divine calling at all—for a divine calling is realizable only in terms of real work within the real world! The papal prohibition of marriage to the clergy, thundered Luther, was "a diabolical doctrine of Antichrist." Indeed, he continued, the Romanistic distinction between the sacred and the secular is false, "inasmuch as all Christians belong to the truly spiritual class; for very truly there is no difference among them, inasmuch as they all hold a sacred office—I Cor. 12 & I Pet. 2." "When you are a believer," he insisted, "even *carnalia* [or physical and fleshly things] and *animalia* [or psychical things] and *officia* [or appointed things] are pleasing to God—whether you eat, or drink, or are vigilant, or sleep: which things pertain merely to the body or to the mind. *All* of these things are matters of faith!" And, he added, "a housemaid too does good works, when

61

she fulfills her calling in faith and does what her mistress asks her to do when she (the maid) cleans out the house and washes and cooks in the kitchen."[25]

It was, however, particularly John Calvin who systematized and elaborated the implications of the Reformation. Calvin repudiated the perverted teachings of the Church of Rome, and set about developing a truly Biblical life and world view based on the absolute sovereignty of God over the whole of life (including culture). For Calvin opposed the Romish concept of ecclesiastical hierarchy with the Scriptural concept of the prophethood, priesthood, and kingship of all believers and their mutual covenantal solidarity; and, like Zwingli, he appreciated the elements of truth even in the works of the unregenerate (namely, in his elaboration of the doctrine of common grace).

Calvin's Biblical views thus had profound implications for the whole of man's culture—particularly in respect of politics, public morality, economics, and education, where Calvin moved for better municipal health laws, employment opportunities, private industrial development, and God-centered academies. For, to Calvin, the development of the heart and the body and the mind, of the arts and the sciences and everything else to the glory of God, was a *vocatio Dei,* or a divine calling. "Philosophy," Calvin wrote to Bucer, "is therefore an excellent gift of God, and learned men in every country who zealously devoted themselves thereto, were influenced by God Himself, so that they would give to the world the information of the knowledge of the truth."[26]

The Thomistic distinction between "secular" manual labor and "sacred" spiritual work was foreign to Calvin's understanding of the

25. Richardson, *The Biblical Doctrine of Work* (London: SCM Press, 1963), p. 36; Holl, *Ges. Aufsätze zur kirchengeschichte* (Tübingen, Germany, 1928), III, 219; Luthardt, *Die Ethik Luthers* (Leipzig, Germany, 1867), p. 98; Luther, *An den Christlichen Adel deutscher Nation* (Halle, Germany: Braune, 1897), p. 7; *Genesis-exegese: Op. Lat.,* ed. Elsperger, VII, 225, and *Pred. Tit.* 2, 13.

26. Calvin, *Letter to Bucer,* as quoted in Potgieter, *Die Verhouding tussen die Teologie en die Filosofie by Calvyn* (Amsterdam: Noord-Hollandse Publishing Co., 1939), p. 192; cf. Lee; *Calvin on the Sciences,* p. 10.

teaching of Holy Scripture. *"All* human labor is of *equal* value; after all, all [Christians] are in the Lord's service, and contribute toward the maintenance of human society," said Calvin.[27] *"All* craftsmen of whatever kind, who serve the needs of men, are *ministers* of God," he added elsewhere,[28] and even "agriculture is *commanded* by God."[29]

After Calvin, who unshakeably asserted that "the fear of the Lord is the beginning of wisdom" (cf. Prov. 1:7), the world would never be the same again. Rome shook to her sacerdotal foundations. Creaturely ecclesiastical imperialism over the whole of life in its usurpation of God's cosmos-embracing Kingdom was beaten back, and the Creator's total authority in every field of man's cultural endeavor was once again proclaimed.

It is surely a remarkable fact that the greatest blossoming of the world's culture has occurred precisely in those very lands where the Gospel of Christ, as understood in its most universal scope, has achieved its greatest triumphs. True, even before the time of Christ, Greece and Rome, Egypt and Babylon, China and India—and, to a lesser extent—even Japan and Central America—did reach a much higher level of cultural development than the then backward nations of Northern and Western Europe, Africa, Northern and Central Asia, Australia, and North and South America. But even the comparative richness of these first-mentioned cultures of the ancient world is very much overshadowed by that of later Europe and the United States. True, the Moslem lands did become the bearers of ancient Greek philosophy and the remarkable mathematical culture of the Arabs during the Dark Ages of Europe; but even then, the considerable influence of the Bible and of Christianity in the formation of Islam must never be forgotten. The fact remains, it is in the Christian countries of the world in general, and in the Protestant countries in particular, that culture (which includes technology) has reached its greatest level of development.

Alongside the study of the Biblical languages Greek and Hebrew and of the Church language Latin, the dead cultures of ancient

27. Calvin, *Opera Omnia*, XXVII, 14.
28. *Ibid.*, XXXVI, 83.
29. *Ibid.*, XXIII, 83.

Greece and Rome were resurrected, and resulted in the Renaissance: art and architecture flourished in Italy, philosophy in France and England. Increasing study of the Bible in Germany and Switzerland led to the Reformation, with its far-reaching religious and political and economic results. As a consequence of the Reformation, we now possess the immortal "soli Deo gloria" music of Johann Sebastian Bach, much of the extensive literature of Northern Europe, and the sphere-sovereign Constitution and the tremendous economic output of the United States of America (which was colonized to a considerable extent by the Pilgrim Fathers with their long-abiding Puritan work ethic). And more recently, to this has been added the gigantic cultural contributions of Kuyper and Dooyeweerd in the Netherlands, and of Stoker and Venter in South Africa.

Often as a direct result of Christian missions, literacy and health programs have been promoted all over the world among the heathen, and only eternity will reveal the extent of the continuing impact and influence of the Gospel of Jesus Christ in the world at large. Even the Far Eastern cultures of India, China, and Japan received a new cultural stimulus as a result of continuing contact with the Christian West during the last two centuries.

Truly, the world's culture has now blossomed (as a result of Christ's incarnation) as never before!

* * * * *

Let us now summarize this chapter on the blossoming of culture, and then draw some cultural directives from it.

First, we noted that Jews and Moslems and even evolutionists and Karl Marx himself have conceded that the earthly life of Jesus Christ and its permanent consequences represent the actual blossoming of the world's cultural history.

Second, we observed that the cultural crisis throughout the Mediterranean world at the time of Christ's advent cried out for the coming of a great Hero to give new cultural direction, and in fact (at least partially) did so acknowledge Jesus as that Hero at His birth.

Third, it was seen that God the Son incarnated Himself as the Second Adam, discoursed about the lilies of the field and the fowl of the air and the beasts of the field and the fishes of the sea with

64

a far greater wisdom than even Solomon ever did, and Himself subdued the earth and the sea and the sky as nobody before Him had ever done.

Fourth, we noted that after Jesus shed His precious blood to save sinners and to restore their culture, the risen Christ's Great Commission also re-enjoins the dominion charter of cultural involvement to the glory of God, and that Christians are raised from their evil and deadness together with Christ in order to have dominion over sin. In principle they sit with Christ in heaven right here and now and thus participate in His continued subduing of the universe.

Fifth, the outpouring of the Holy Spirit at Pentecost did not cancel but rather sanctified and renewed the pluriform culture of man, and even today that indwelling Spirit not only causes Christians to preach about Christ's cosmos-embracing Kingship with power, but also causes them to live in all the many spheres thereof in practice too.

Sixth, we saw that the early Church long ago struggled to achieve the right cultural balance. There were erroneous differences of opinion as to the nature of Christ's Kingdom among some of the Hebrew Christians, the Corinthian Christians, and the Thessalonian Christians respectively. Later, Clement was too uncritical of the sinful quality of worldly culture, Tertullian was too uncritical of culture as such, and although Augustine made a gigantic step forward in the historical development of the Christian concept of culture, his effort was still later largely neutralized by Thomas Aquinas, who dichotomously segregated the supposedly sacred Church from supposedly secular culture.

And seventh, we saw that the Protestant Reformation fortunately in large measure corrected this, when Luther and especially Calvin proclaimed the kingship of Christ over the *whole* of life and established the formal equality of the value before God of all godly professions and cultural activity, as a result of which during the subsequent centuries the development of culture throughout the world received its major stimulus.

* * * * *

What, then, can we learn from all the above? What permanently valuable cultural directives can we extract from our brief study of the historical development of Christian cultural attitudes?

First, we should learn that it is only the advent of Christ and the dynamic development of early Christianity which checked the further deterioration of the cultures of the ancient world by Christianizing the erstwhile culturally depraved heathen Roman Empire as the repository of the world's culture. And similarly, it is only the powerful expansion of a consistent form of Christianity today which can save our present culture too from collapse.

Second, we must understand that the culture-avoiding stance of Tertullian and the Anabaptists (and even of the later Pietists) is perhaps even more dangerous than the opposite error of the wholesale adoption of worldly culture as in Clement, Origen, and even in late mediaeval Romanism. As the Belgic Confession states: "For this reason we reject the Anabaptists and other seditious people, and in general *all those who reject the higher powers and magistrates* and would subvert justice, *introduce community of goods,* and confound that decency and good order which God has established among men," for "it is the bounden duty of every one, of whatever state, quality, or condition he may be, *to subject himself to the magistrates; to pay tribute, show due honor and respect* to them, and to obey them in all things which are not repugnant to the Word of God; and pray for them, that God may rule and guide them in all their ways and *that we may lead a quiet and peaceable life in all godliness and honesty."*[30]

And third, we should value our cultural heritage and continue to build on the teachings of the Bible, of Augustine, of Calvin, of the Puritans, of the Pilgrim Fathers, and of Kuyper, thus promoting the further blossoming of culture, as enjoined to all men in the great dominion charter given to Adam, to "be fruitful, and multiply, and replenish the earth, and subdue it" (Gen. 1:28). For, as the sixteenth-century Second Helvetic Confession so correctly states: "Children are to be brought up by the parents in the fear of the Lord, and parents are to provide for their children, remembering the saying of the apostle: 'If anyone does not provide for his relatives, he has

---

30. *Belgic Confession,* art. 36; cf. I Tim. 2:1-2.

66

disowned the faith and is worse than an unbeliever' (I Tim. 5:8). But especially they should teach their children honest trades or professions by which they may support themselves. They should keep them from idleness and in all these things instill in them true faith in God, lest through a lack of confidence or too much security or filthy greed they become dissolute and achieve no success. And it is most certain that those works which are done by parents in true faith by way of domestic duties and the management of their households are in God's sight holy and truly good works. They are *no less pleasing to God* than prayers, fasting and almsgiving."[31]

* * * * *

Thus has culture blossomed; and may you and I cause it to blossom still further! For as the great South African culturologist C. N. Venter has truly remarked, the Christian believer's "cultural vocation and ultimate cultural destination consists of him faithfully executing his baptismal promises and living out in practice the faith he professes in his *culture* (that is, in his daily task and religious service of God [*Godsdiens*]), in accordance with the demands of a pure, continually reforming tradition, on the basis of the covenantal promises of God."[32]

"And *whatsoever* ye do in word or *deed,* do *all* in the Name of the Lord Jesus, giving thanks to God and the Father by Him" (Col. 3:17). "As every man hath received the gift, even so minister the same one to another, as good stewards of the manifold grace of God. If any man speak, let him speak as the Oracles of God; if any man minister, let him do it as of the ability which God giveth: that God in *all* things may be glorified through Jesus Christ, to Whom be praise and *dominion* for ever and ever! Amen" (I Pet. 4:10).

---

31. *Second Helvetic Confession,* chap. XXIX.
32. Venter, *'n Calvinistiese Kultuurbeskouing, 1969–1970,* in *Koers* XXXVII nr. 3 en 4 (Potchefstroom, South Africa: Potchefstroom Herald), Feb. 1970.

IV

THE FRUITS OF CULTURE

What is the ultimate purpose of culture? Where is it heading, and what is its future?

According to Karl Marx's *Critique of the Gotha Program:* "In a higher phase of communist society, after the enslaving subordination of the individual to the division of labor, and therewith also the antithesis between mental and physical labor, has vanished; after labor has become not only a means of life, but life's prime want; after the productive forces have also increased with the all-round development of the individual, and all the springs of co-operative wealth flow more abundantly—only then can the narrow horizon of bourgeois right be crossed in its entirety and society inscribe on its banners: From each according to his ability, to each according to his needs!"[1]

However, the humanistic futurologists Kahn and Wiener, in their massive study on *The Year 2000,* in discussing man's increasing Faustian power over nature (including man), are considerably more restrained: "Man is developing enormous power to change his own environment—not only the outside world, but also his own physiological and intrapsychic situation. The prevailing secular humanist view is that this is 'progress'—and we would agree that it would be no more desirable than feasible to attempt to halt the process permanently, or to reverse it. Yet this very power over nature threatens to become a force of nature that is itself out of control, as the social framework of action obscures and thwarts not only the human objectives of all the striving for 'achievement' and 'advance-

---

1. Cf. Marx and Engels, *Selected Works,* II, 163.

ment,' but also the various inarticulate or ideological reactions against the process. In the final decades of this century, we shall have the technological and economic power to change the world radically, but probably not get very much ability to restrain our strivings, let alone understand or control the results of the changes we will be making. But if we cannot learn not only to take full advantage of our increasing technological success, but also cope with its dangerous responsibilities, we may only have thrown off one set of chains—nature-imposed—for another, ostensibly man-made, but in a deeper sense, as Faust learned, also imposed by nature."[2]

And as the publisher's blurb tells us about Ritchie Calder's *After the Seventh Day—the World Man Created*: "The author maintains that technology, more than wars and kings, has shaped history. And he points out that now our technology has come close to conquering the last physical and climatic barriers to a workable civilization; now we can create the world we want—make it a garden or a desert, shape it or crush it."[3]

Prediction is, of course, always a risky business. As Kahn and Wiener themselves wrote in their book *The Year 2000* (itself written in 1967): "Unfortunately, the uncertainties in any study looking more than five or ten years ahead are usually so great that the simple chain of prediction, policy change, and new prediction is very tenuous indeed."[4] However, unlike any other book, the Christian Bible does delineate the *general* trend of future events, and even of cultural expectations, if not the *specific* details. Accordingly, it is to the Bible again that we must turn, if we are to understand the nature of the possibility of the future fruits of culture.

* * * * *

In this chapter on the fruits of culture, then, we shall examine the teachings of the Bible and Bible-believing scholars relative to the future of culture. First, we shall see that the basic doctrinal teachings of Scripture indicate an essential continuity in cultural develop-

2. *The Year 2000: A Framework for Speculation on the Next Thirty-three Years* (New York: Macmillan, 1967), pp. 409, 412.
3. Calder, *op. cit.*, p. 1.
4. Kahn and Wiener, *op. cit*, p. 1.

ment from the past through the present into the future (and even beyond the grave). Second, we shall point out that leading Christian thinkers down through Church history have recognized this indication. Third, we shall illustrate the practical importance here and now of recognizing the cultural nature of life in the world to come. Fourth, we shall show the connection between cultural life as it is here and now on earth and as it is here and now in heaven. Fifth, we shall indicate the probable future of culture here on our present earth prior to Christ's second coming. And lastly, we shall attempt to describe the ultimate consummation of culture on the new earth to come after the final judgment.

*　*　*　*　*

In the first place, then, the basic doctrinal teachings of the Bible themselves indicate an essential continuity in the cultural development from the past and through the present and into the future (and even beyond the grave).

"In the beginning God created the heaven and the earth. And the earth was without form and void" (Gen. 1:1-2). However, "God Himself that formed the earth and made it; He hath established it, He created it not in vain, He formed it to be *inhabited*" (Isa. 45:18). So He caused it to become inhabited with minerals and plants and animals in six days, preparing it for the advent of man who would use these commodities. For thus saith the Lord: "I have made the earth, and created *man* upon it" (Isa. 45:12), and God "hath made of one blood all nations of men *for to dwell* on all the face of the earth . . . that they should seek the Lord" (Acts 17:26-27).

Moreover (as Popma and Jager have pointed out),[5] none of the new works divinely manufactured on the later days of the formation week of this world (such as the birds and animals and man) cancelled out the creatures made on the earlier days of the divine formation week (such as air, land, and plants), but only sanctified them further alongside of and in interdependence with the new items

<hr>

5. Cf. chap. 1, notes 29, 30, above. Cf. too Popma, *Levensbeschouwing*, II, 90 and III, 191; and Jager, *Het Eeuwige Leven* (Kampen: J. H. Kok, 1962), p. 403.

created later during those six divine working days (Gen. 1:3-31). And many of these creatures (such as land, plants, animals, and man) will still be found on the new earth to come (as we will shortly demonstrate below).

Again, our Savior at His incarnation did not bring a "new" earthly body with Him down from heaven, but "inherited" an "old" (though sinless) body from His mother and from all her ancestors "according to the flesh" (Rom. 1:3), and, inasmuch as He will still have that earthly body at His second coming, it hardly seems likely that the advent of the future eighth day of the Lord will cancel out the true products of His (and our) cultural activity either. For the good products of man's works now being performed during God's great seventh day (which is co-extensive with the history of man himself, and on which great seventh day God is resting in order to make the universe further—through *man*),[5] shall ever endure throughout the future everlasting Day of the Lord, even as our *enjoyment* of the cumulative fruits of our cultural works rendered during the six days of labor every working week here and now, is in no way destroyed or curtailed by the arrival of the weekly sabbaths of our present lives!

Of course, it is perfectly true that no *personal* continued existence of plants and animals in the next life is taught by Scripture—for personality is an attribute of spiritual beings alone (namely, of God, angels, and men). However, a *genetical* continued existence of flora and fauna *is* indeed taught, in contradistinction to the transmutation doctrine of evolutionism![6] Moreover, *Christ Himself*—while speaking precisely of the *everlasting* covenant! (Matt. 26:28; Heb. 13:20)—unreservedly taught the eschatological continued existence of at least *the vine* in the hereafter, for He promised to drink the fruit of the vine with His disciples *anew* in the Kingdom of His Father (Matt. 26:29; cf. Isa. 25:6-9), which at least partially refers

---

6. Kuyper, *Van de Voleinding*, I, 490ff. The eschatological continued existence of prehistoric and other extinct genuses does indeed create an apparent problem, but here again Abraham Kuyper has offered us an acceptable explanation in pointing out that the development of the universe does indeed manifest an upward tendency toward ever greater refinement!

to the life to come, as pointed out by both Kuyper[7] and Berkouwer.[8] And *that* implies that at least some members of the present vegetable kingdom will still be thriving on the new earth to come!

However, inasmuch as wine or "the fruit of the vine" is a human *cultural* product (cf. Gen. 9:1-7, 20-21a) of the natural vine which we have just seen will still grow on the new earth to come, our Savior's words imply that viticulture (and therefore culture!) too will continue there and then. Moreover, Christ teaches us in the parable of the talents that whatever we honestly gain here and now on earth will continue to hold for all eternity too! (Matt. 25:13-30). For the eschatological perfection of *culture* as the work of *personal* men— *even more* than the eschatological perfection of *nature* with its *impersonal* creatures—flows forth unbrokenly from God's creation and by way of His still unfolding maintenance of the world at large and especially of the world of man and *all* that it contains: for the creation and unfolding maintenance and eschatological goal of all things form one unbreakable triune chain.

Indeed, Isaiah chapters eleven, thirty-five, and sixty-five—although in a certain sense right now being fulfilled between Christ's first and second comings, and although containing spiritual elements intertwined with the material elements—*also* clearly imply that the originally created and currently unfolding vegetable and animal kingdoms in their relation to man will still be found (although in their then perfected state) on the new earth yet to come. And in the light of Revelation, chapter fourteen, (where we are told that the believers' works do follow them after their death), it is not easy to see how the present earthly works of the Christian botanist or zoologist *can* follow them, *unless* there be both a botanical and a zoological order in the hereafter![9]

Now it was precisely to encourage the production of such good works that God in the first place gave our first parents the great cultural commission: "Be fruitful and multiply, and replenish the earth,

---

7. *Ibid.*, I, 490.

8. Berkouwer, *De Wederkomst van Christus* (Kampen: J. H. Kok, 1961), I, 294, n. 143.

9. Kuyper, *De Gemeene Gratie*, 4th ed. (Kampen: J. H. Kok), I, 468. See too the text at notes 27 and 28 below and our Third Appendix below.

and subdue it: and have dominion over the fish of the sea, and over the fowl of the air, and over every living thing that moveth upon the earth" (Gen. 1:28). And even though man has subsequently sinned against God, God shall still realize His eternal purpose! For elect man or "Israel shall be saved in the Lord with an everlasting salvation: ye shall not be ashamed nor confounded, world without end!" (Isa. 45:17).

Indeed, if Adam had remained faithful to the covenant of works (Gen. 1:26-28; Hos. 6:7 margin), he would never have died, and would ultimately have been translated from the losable everlasting life with which he was created into the unlosable everlasting life which was promised him if obedient to the covenant (Matt. 19:4-6, 16-21 cf. I Cor. 15:37-53). This would have marked his entry into the very sabbath rest of God, or the state of glory (Gen. 1:28–2:3; Heb. 4:3-4, 9-11), whereby the Day of the Lord would have arrived and creation would have been perfected (Mal. 3:17; 4:1-5; Matt. 22:30). *But even then, Adam would still have had a body in glory,* inasmuch as Jesus Christ *the Second Adam now has a body in glory.* The unfallen Adam's body *would* have been glorified at the successful end of his period of probation here on earth (cf. I Cor. 15:45-51)— as indeed it yet *will* be, through the merits of the Second Adam Jesus Christ!

Furthermore, seeing that Adam would always have had a body, it is obvious that Adam would also have acquired and retained all those bodily produced permanent cultural products which the resurrected Second Adam had. Indeed, the nature of Christ's resurrection body is extremely significant in this respect. For Christ was the Second *Adam* (I Cor. 15:22, 45-47), and *the resurrected Christ was the heavenly perfected Second Adam* (Heb. 2:5-10; 4:3-14). Accordingly, inasmuch as we are informed that the resurrected Second Adam wore beautiful clothes (Rev. 1:13-18; cf. Matt. 17:2, 9), ate culturally prepared food (Luke 24:30, 42-43), and Himself labored to make a fire of coals to cook food for others (John 21:9-14), we can certainly assume that the first Adam—like all of his elect descendants on the new earth to come—in spite of all changes he and his culture would undoubtedly have undergone (I Cor. 15:51; 6:13

cf. Matt. 22:30), once he had been "resurrected" or rather translated from loseable life to unloseable life, would similarly have worn beautiful clothes, continued to eat culturally prepared food, and labored for others, as did the resurrected Second *Adam*. In fact, it is perhaps highly significant that when Mary Magdalene first saw the resurrected Second Adam, she thought that He was the *gardener* (John 20:15)—and, as Rudyard Kipling once remarked in one of his poems: *"Adam* was a gardener," and "the Glory of the Garden it shall *never* pass away!"[10]

Moreover, the essentially human nature and human products which the resurrected Son of man had, *we too* (both as the sons of Adam and as the sons of the Son of man and Second Adam) shall have at *our* resurrection (Phil. 3:21; I John 3:2). For the re-embodied resurrection saints will *also* have food (Rev. 2:7; 22:2), clothes (Rev. 6:9-11; 7:9, 13), and culture (Gen. 2:9-19; Rev. 21:24-26). Indeed, the tree of life in the garden of Eden is unfolded by way of the tree of death near the garden of Gethsemene into the whole grove of trees of life in the garden of Paradise-to-come!

Cultural development, then, exhibits a *basic continuity* from the past through the present and into the future beyond the grave, in spite of the elements of change involved in its growth and even in spite of the dislocating and sometimes even catastrophic impact of sin on cultural development.

* * * * *

Second, the essential continuity between both nature and culture in this life and in the next has also been recognized by leading Christian thinkers down throughout Church history.

The Christian Church as a whole and the Western Church in particular has always emphasized that the nature of the hereafter is both material and spiritual, and that saved man will continue to exercise his dominion charter on the new earth to come, as already suggested at the end of the first century A.D. in the Epistle of (Pseudo-)Barnabas (ch. VI). In general, it was only the later idealistic-spiritualistic

---

10. Rudyard Kipling, "The Glory of the Garden," from *The History of England* (Clarendon Press), in *Twenty Poems from Rudyard Kipling* (London: Methuen & Co., Ltd., 1942), p. 22.

Eastern Church[11] and antimaterial heretics such as the Gnostics, Docetists, and Anabaptists who (like the Modernists!) sometimes treated eschatology (and indeed the whole of theology) in a one-sided spiritualistic way.[12]

As regards the Church in the West before the Reformation, we refer to the great doctors of the Church—such as *Augustine*[13] (in his second, anti-Origenistic period!), *Jerome* and *Thomas Aquinas*[13]—who all emphasized the materiality of the future life to come.

With reference to the Church in the West at the time of the Reformation, we refer to Luther and Calvin in particular.

Luther recognized the materiality of the world to come of the future, where he declared, "If our parents had not sinned in Paradise, the world would never have perished; however, inasmuch as they fell into sin, and all of us after them, the whole creation too had to suffer because of us, and has also been subjected to vanity and disturbance for the sake of our sins. For the nearly six thousand years it has now been standing, it has remained subjected to the condemned world, and has had to serve it with all of its abilities. But when God amasses it all together, the creation itself will once again be purified and renewed (as St. Peter too teaches in II Pet. 3). The sun is heartily longing for that Day when it will again be polished up (*ausgeputzt werden*) and will serve the blessed alone with its light. The earth is also longing together with every creature for that Day when it will be changed and renewed together with them. For this cause the whole creation cries out: Oh, oh, when will the end of the suffering draw near, and the glory of the children of God begin?"[14]

Calvin too, in spite of his great eschatological sobriety for fear of neo-scholastic speculation, was nevertheless unshakable in his belief

---

11. Berkhof, *The History of Christian Doctrine* (Grand Rapids: Eerdmans, 1959), pp. 273, 274.

12. Cf. *Belgic Confession*, arts. 18, 37.

13. Cf. Berkhof, *op. cit.*, pp. 273, 274; Bruchrucker, "Heaven," art. in *Schaff-Herzog Encyclopaedia* (New York: Funk & Wagnalls, 1891), II; Jansen, "Hemelleven," and Kaajan, "Hemelsch," both in *Christelijke Encyclopaedie*, II.

14. Luther, *Church Postille*, ed. Bahnmair, II, 363.

that eternal life would also have a material side. ". . . the body in. which we shall rise, will be the same as at present in respect of substance," he wrote,[15] and again:[16] "Shall the lower *animals,* and inanimate creatures themselves, even *wood and stone,* as conscious of their present vanity, *long for* the final resurrection, that they may with the sons of God be delivered from vanity (Rom. 8:19) . . .?"— namely, if they themselves have no interest in continuing to exist (albeit in glorified form) after man's resurrection? And elsewhere, when some inquirers asked of Calvin,[17] "to what end the world is to be repaired . . .?" he answered, ". . . that independent of *use,* there will be so much pleasantness in the very *sight,* . . . that this happiness will far surpass all the means of enjoyment which are now afforded. . . . *fruition,* pure and free from defect . . . is the summit of happiness." And where others asked whether "*impurities* in *metals* will have no existence at the restitution?" Calvin answered, "I . . . concede this to them, yet I expect with Paul a *reparation* of those defects which first began with sin, and on account of which the whole creation groaneth and travaileth with pain (Romans 8:22). . . . When Scripture so highly extols the blessing of offspring, it refers to the progress by which God is constantly urging nature forward to its *goal* in perfection."

"Of the elements of the world," Calvin stated in his Commentary on II Peter 3:10, on *the future renewal of our present heaven and earth,* "I should only say this one thing, that they are to be consumed, *only that they may be renovated,* their substance still remaining the same, as may easily be gathered from Romans 8:21 and from other passages." And on Romans 8:19f. he commented that the "obedience in all things . . . springs from hope," for God has "implanted inwardly the hope of renovation" into "the alacrity of the *sun and moon,* and of *all the stars* in their constant courses, . . . the *earth's* obedience in bringing forth *fruits,* . . . the unwearied motion of the *air,* . . . [and] the prompt tendency to flow in *water*" (cf. Rev.

---

15. Calvin, *Institutes of the Christian Religion,* III:25:8.
16. *Ibid.,* III:9:5.
17. *Ibid.,* III:25:11.

22:1-2), for at that future time, *"all creatures* shall be renewed, . . . , *beasts* as well as *plants* and *metals,"* for "there is no element and *no part of the world which,* being touched, as it were, with a sense of its present misery, *does not intensely hope for a resurrection."*

As regards the Church in the West after the Reformation, after a long period of subsequent decline as a result of formalism, rationalism, pietism, and spiritualism, Abraham Kuyper rejected the spiritualistic marginal rendering of the eschatological parts (such as Isaiah chapters 11 and 65 and Revelation chapter 22) of the States-General translation of the Dutch Bible as "too one-sided," because these marginal renderings "betrayed the tendency from the very beginning to ascribe significance to practically *only the spiritual* enjoyments in the eternal glory which is to come. . . . Hence there is nothing puzzling or strange in the fact that at the end of the prophecies of the book of Revelation, mention is made of *a city,* in contradistinction to *the country* surrounding that city. . . . . It can mean nothing less than that the all-embracing difference between *agricultural* life and centralized *urban* life will continue *even in the hereafter."*[18] "Now we should be sober and careful here," he wrote elsewhere,[19] "but yet it will not .do to discover merely a symbolical expression of the spiritual in all this. Together with a life in the state of glory, a *world* is also required in which one must live, according to both body and soul. . . . From Romans 8:19 this appears to be the case of *the animal world* in what is revealed there about 'the creature,' and it further appears that a much higher excellency is then attributed to the tree of life than the vegetable kingdom possesses on this present earth [now]. . . . And even though this is *in part* symbolical, nevertheless there is the indication of a much higher development of power in the *vegetable kingdom* than is known here."

In the Foreword to this book (*Van de Voleinding* or *Concerning the Consummation*), Dr. *H. H. Kuyper* wrote that its author, his father Dr. Abraham Kuyper, proceeded "from the Counsel of God

---

18. Kuyper, *Van de Voleinding,* IV, 384, 395, 400.
19. *Ibid.,* I, 495. Cf. too his *De Gemeene Gratie,* I, 481-482, where Kuyper agrees that the parable of the talents (Matt. 25) teaches that our (honest!) present earthly gains will abide with us for all eternity too.

in which this consummation is predetermined; and then he shows how this consummation applies not only to man and his salvation, but embraces *the whole creation* in its organic context—heaven and earth, man and angels, animals and plants. . . . The complaint which frequently recurs in this work, namely that our old Reformed writers treated this all-important subject in a rather stepmotherly fashion and that all kinds of sectarian spirits have mastered it precisely on account of this lack of interest on the part of the Church, is not exaggerated."[20]

So too Kuyper's other son, the celebrated theologian *Dr. Abraham Kuyper, Jr.,* also pointed out that Romans 8:19ff. clearly teaches "that *the creation* longs for the revelation of the children of God [and] that *the creation too* shall be liberated from the bondage of corruption. . . . Here the ideas concerning glorification run co-extensively with the ideas concerning the curse, for the creation in its entirety—thus plants and animals too—groan under the curse. . . . Why should the plants and animals be excluded from the liberation of the creation, seeing that they too belong to the creation? And so there are sufficient reasons here to place 'cursed for Adam's sake' over against 'glorified for Christ's sake.' "[21] .

Bavinck too has something to say: "The whole creation . . . is liberated . . ., and the *vegetable and plant world* will also participate therein, Isaiah 11:6f, and 65:21f. The New Jerusalem which is now above and indicates the city where God dwells with his people, then descends to the earth, Revelation 21:2."[22] *Karl Dijk,* perhaps the leading modern Reformed eschatologian, also confirmed this view when he wrote:[23] "The *entire* material world thus participates in the renewal which God brings to life. . . . The whole of earthly life is rescued from vanity; it is exalted to a glory which surpasses the

---

20. H. H. Kuyper, in Dr. A. Kuyper, *Van de Voleinding,* I, 7, 8.

21. A. Kuyper, Jr., *Van de Heiligmaking, van de Heerlijkmaking, en van het Rijk der Heerlijkheid* (Delft, Netherlands: Meinema, 1935), p. 364.

22. Bavinck, *Handleiding bij het Onderwijs van den Christelijken Godsdienst* (Kampen: J. H. Kok, 1932); cf. too his *Gereformeerde Dogmatiek* (Kampen: J. H. Kok, 1930), IV, 701-702.

23. Dijk, *De Leer der Laasten Dingen,* in Berkouwer en Toornvliet, *Het Dogma der Kerk* (Groningen, Netherlands: Jan Haan, 1949), p. 600.

beauty of Eden. . . . Matter too shall be glorified by God through the power of the work of Christ, and the promise of the *realm of peace* will be fulfilled, about which Isaiah sung his song: the *desert shall blossom* like a *rose* (Isa. 11 and 35); . . . *all* culture, *all* science and art—although completely purified and celestially sanctified—shall together constitute the glory of the city of God; *city and garden* will coincide, for the tree of life *blossoms* there."

Even the Barthian *Eduard Thurneysen* recognized this obvious doctrine when he wrote: "The world into which we shall come at the second coming of Christ, will therefore be no other world. It will be this world, these heavens, this earth—but all passed away and become new. These *forests*, these *fields*, these *cities*, these *streets*—it will be these *people* who will be the theater of redemption."[24] "And one may not leave in the shade," added *Berkouwer*,[25] "that which is inextricably connected with the resurrection of the flesh, and which is portrayed for us as the *life* . . . [namely that] it will be *very earthly*."

The basic continuity of cultural life in this life and in the next is thus clearly recognized by all these leading theologians.

* * * * *

Third, what is the practical importance to us here and now of knowing that there is to be a cultural life in the world to come too?

A *de*materialized and *de*culturalized presentation of the life in the world to come, is not only unscriptural, but in our opinion also provokes a material*istic* representation of a future earthly millennium as an unavoidable reaction thereagainst. Material-spiritual man, the simple yet unpietized Christian, feels instinctively that the hereafter or at 'east part of it must somehow include a strongly material aspect too, in order to be true to reality. A non-material future *Nirvana* as opposed to a material-spiritual new earth to come, is the expectation of *Buddhism*—and *not* of Christianity!

Even Jewish apocalyptics thirst for and correctly expect a material world to come. If Karl Marx had only found it among the hypersoteriological, ultraspiritualistic Christians of his own day, he might

---

24. Thurneysen, *Christus und seine Zeiten* (Munich, 1931), p. 209.
25. Berkouwer, *De Wederkomst van Christus*, I, 294, 299.

have remained with them, instead of trying to realize his own materi-
alistically exaggerated and unfortunately secularized and atheistic yet
nevertheless material realm of peace under future communism! And
a more true-to-reality, down-to-earth Christianity might also have converted the great Chassidic Jewish philosopher Martin Buber too![26]

Furthermore, we would agree with *De Bondt*[27] that a material expectation of the hereafter is of great importance precisely in respect
of our present life's work, our career, in this world here and now:
"The botanist engaged in investigating the secrets of organic life may
say: 'On the *new* earth I shall be busy in a vegetable world without
curse, with an understanding no longer darkened. That must be
wonderful! But even now I am able to notice *something* of the
mystery of God's work.' "

So, together with *Abraham Kuyper*, we too would lament the
spiritualistic and unbalanced presentation of the new earth yet to
come on the part of those who would dematerialize the future life:
"Oh, they naturally believe that there will be a resurrection of the
flesh; for it is taught so definitely. But they do not rejoice about it,
they do not exalt therein! It might just as well not be there. The
over-spiritual Christians would even like to demand that it be omitted.
But in that case, what would they do with 'the new earth'? A new
earth which (to suit *their* expectations!) would have to possess a
new (dematerialized) nature, a nature in which no rose of Sharon
would be allowed to blossom, and in which no lark would be allowed
to sing its song to God"![28]

As Archbishop *William Temple* once said: "Christianity is the most
materialistic of all great religions."[29] For "the Word was made *flesh*,
and dwelt among us" (John 1:14). So too the Belgic Confession

---

26. *Ibid.*, p. 290.
27. De Bondt, *De Algemene Genade*, in Berkouwer en Toornvliet, *op. cit.*,
p. 283. See too Third Appendix, below.
28. Kuyper, *Van de Voleinding*, I, 488.
29. Temple, *Readings in St. John's Gospel*, as quoted in Richardson,
Christian Economics (Houston: St. Thomas Press, 1966), p. 7. We ourselves
would prefer to say that Christianity is the most *material* (not materialistic) of
all great religions, but Temple's point is nevertheless well made and well
taken—F. N. Lee.

rightly rejects the heresy of the Anabaptists who deny that Christ took on sin-weakened yet sinless human flesh from His earthly mother (Art. 18, cf. Rom. 8:3), and the Heidelberg Catechism insists that He rose from the dead in the *same* earthly body in which He was crucified so that in Him "we have *our flesh* in heaven" (Q. 45-49; John 20:25-27); and "We know that when He shall appear, *we* shall be *like* Him; for we shall *see* Him as He *is* (I John 3:2). "For our conversation [or walk of life] is in heaven: from whence also we look for the Saviour, the Lord Jesus Christ: Who shall change our vile [or sin-weakened] body, that it may be[come] fashioned like unto His glorious [and still material!] body" (Phil. 3:21).

And for *this* reason, the Christian Church of all ages confesses in the Apostles' Creed every Sunday: "I believe in the resurrection of the *body,* and an everlasting life!"[30]

* * * * *

Fourth, let us look at the connection between cultural life as it is here and now on earth, and as it is here and now in heaven. For it is precisely in *heaven* that the (deceased) elders of the Christian Church do sing: "Thou are worthy, O Lord, to receive glory and honor and power: for Thou hast created *all* things, and for Thy pleasure they *are,* and were *created!*" (Rev. 4:1, 10-11).

The heavens declare the glory of God (Ps. 19:1), and there the Lord has prepared His throne, Whose Kingdom ruleth over all. There His angels do His commandments, hearkening unto the voice of His word, and there all His works bless Him in all places of His dominion (Ps. 103:19-22). So much so, that Jesus said we are to pray for the coming of the Kingdom here on earth, even as it has already come in its sinless perfection in heaven above (Isa. 14:

---

30. It should be noted that Presbyterians usually append this Apostles' Creed at the end of the Westminster Shorter Catechism and that Reformed Christians have inserted it as an integral part of the Heidelberg Catechism, Q. 22-59. Cf. *Die Drie Formuliere van Enigheid* (Cape Town: Dutch Reformed Church Publishers, n.d.), pp. 33-40; *The Subordinate Standards and Other Authoritative Documents of the Free Church of Scotland* (Edinburgh: Offices of the Free Church of Scotland, 1933), pp. 249-250; *The Constitution of the Bible Presbyterian Church* (Collingswood, N. J.: The Independent Board for Presbyterian Home Missions, 1959), pp. 120-123.

12-15; Rev. 12:7-9), especially since He as the Son of man has gone to the Father's house with the many mansions to prepare a place for us (John 14:2 cf. 3:13). Until He calls us there at the hour of our death, however, we are to work hard at our cultural tasks here on earth in our Father's business (cf. Luke 2:49), laboring so that we may then, temporarily without our earthly bodies (II Cor. 5:1-8), enter into that heavenly rest from our earthly labors, until our works do follow us (Rev. 14:13).

That Father's house with the many mansions is, in fact, a heavenly city (Heb. 11:13-16), the city of the living God and the heavenly Jerusalem (Heb. 12:22-23), the city which hath foundations, whose Builder and Maker is God (Heb. 11:10). There Jesus dwells as the Son of man, crowned with glory and honor (Heb. 2:9-10; 5:8-9), seated on His throne of grace (Heb. 4:10-16). There He ever prays for His people (Heb. 7:25), ministering in the heavenly sanctuary (Heb. 8:1-5) for the benefit of the citizens of heaven (Phil. 3:20-21) like Moses and Elijah (Matt. 17:1-5; II Pet. 1:16-18), until He brings all those citizens (II Thess. 4:14) and the heavenly city of the New Jerusalem with Him down to earth at the end of history (Rev. 21:1-2, 10).

Right now, however, although heaven is a place of rest from our present earthly labors in the toilsome sweat of our face (Gen. 3:17-19; 5:29), it is by no means a place of inactivity! To the contrary, there God's children continue to *work* for the Lord, albeit in a completely enjoyable manner. For there they reign with Him (Rev. 20:4 cf. Eph. 2:6) and serve Him (Rev. 7:9, 15), are fed by Him (Rev. 7:9, 16-17), and are clothed by Him (Rev. 6:10-11; 7:13-14). There they remember their earthly works (Rev. 6:10; 7:13-14), and there they eagerly await the Christianization of the world here below (Rev. 6:9-11; 15:1-4). But above all, there they worship[31] the Triune God and the Prime Author of all human culture, and there they ceaselessly sing His praises![32]

And as they, like the angels (cf. I Pet. 1:12), desire to look down

31. Rev. 4:1, 8-11; 5:11-14; 6:10; 7:11-17; 15:7f.
32. Rev. 4:7-8; 5:9; 7:9-10, 15; 14:2, 13; 15:1, 3; 19:2f.

at the events transpiring here on earth (Rev. 15:1-4; 6:9-11), we can almost hear them pray: "Thy will be done, O Father, there on earth, as it is in heaven!"

* * * * *

Fifth, then, let us next look at the probable future of cultural life here on our present earth between now and the final judgment.

Here and now on this present earth, said Jesus, we are to do business or to occupy until He comes (Luke 19:13) and to work for the coming of His Kingdom here on earth even as it is right now in heaven (Matt. 6:10). In one sense His Kingdom has *already* come, for He has already established it here on earth (Matt. 4:17; Luke 17:20-21), and we enter it at the moment of our regeneration (John 3:3-5; Col. 1:13). In this sense, culture has already reached its goal in the incarnation of the God of culture Himself in the earthly life and heavenly exaltation of the man Christ Jesus as the Second Adam. In another sense, however, the Kingdom has not yet expanded to its maximum pre-ordained limits. And in this sense it is only after the seventh angel of the book of Revelation sounds his trumpet, that great voices in heaven shall say: "The kingdoms of this world are become the kingdoms of our Lord, and of His Christ; and He shall reign for ever and ever!" (Rev. 11:15).

Yet between these two times—the time of Christ's resurrection and the time of the future Christianization of the kingdoms of *this* (!) world—Christ is not dead, but liveth and is alive for evermore (Rev. 1:18). For Christ has risen from the dead, and God has (in principle) subjected everything under Jesus' feet! And when everything has been subjected to Him completely (in practice too), "then cometh the end, when He shall have delivered up the Kingdom to God, even the Father; when He shall have put down all rule and all authority and power. For He must reign, till He hath put all enemies under His feet. . . . And when all things shall be subdued unto Him, then shall the Son also Himself be subjected unto Him that put all things under Him, that God may be all in all" (I Cor. 15:24-28).

At present, between Christ's ascension and His second coming, the living Savior is expanding His human dominion—His dominion which commenced at His birth, which was completed in principle at His death and resurrection and ascension, and which will be consummated in practice and completely exhibited at His second coming. And at present, this constantly expanding dominion of the living Christ must be exhibited here on earth too. For Christ not only lives as Head of the Church in heaven, but by the power of His indwelling Spirit He also lives here beneath in the people of God of all ages as His earthly body—world without end! (Eph. 1:10, 20-23; 3:20-21). And He lives on earth here and now not only in the Church as an institute, but also in the Church in her non-institutional form as an organism—as the body of Christ in the broader societal spheres in which the people of the God of all culture are (or should be!) attempting to purify art and science and philosophy and literature from all their sinful stains by the grace of God—even as the world and all its culture steadily moves forward down through the centuries toward its *consummation*.

For as we all work hard to expand God's reign here on earth even in the sphere of culture, the consummation steadily draws nearer—the consummation even of all *culture*. At the moment, the whole creation (and therefore all culture too) has been made subject to vanity or nothingness; the whole creation groaneth and travaileth in pain together until now—while it waits with earnest expectation for the manifestation of the sons of God, in the hope that creation itself shall also be delivered from the bondage of corruption into the glorious liberty of the children of God (Rom. 8:19-22). But until then, we Christians are called by God to proclaim an antinihilistic cultural optimism, an optimism amidst and despite all of the sometimes discouraging environmental circumstances, an optimism rooted in the Eternal God and His sure future even for the culture of this His cosmos!

Throughout the course of history, we witness God's periodic judgments over human cultures, followed by mighty Christian revivals. Right at the very end of history, however, it would seem that culture will again degenerate—though not for long (Rev. 12:12; 20:3, 7f.). We cannot know whether the present degeneration of culture will be the final one, but we do know that a final one will one day come.

And then, something similar to the international cosmopolitan city of Babylon of old (cf. Gen. 11; Jer. 51; Dan. 1-5) recurs, and quickly reaches the zenith of its perverted culture (Rev. 18:1-3). But in one single hour God shall strike her with His judgment. "And the merchants of the earth shall weep and mourn over her; for no man buyeth their merchandise any more: the merchandise of gold, and silver, and precious stones, and of pearls, and fine linen, and purple, and silk, and scarlet, and all thyine wood, and all manner vessels of ivory, and all manner vessels of most precious wood, and of brass, and iron, and marble, and cinnamon, and odours, and ointments, and frankincense, and wine, and oil, and fine flour, and wheat, and beasts, and sheep, and horses, and chariots, and slaves, and souls of men. . . . And the voice of harpers, and musicians, and of pipers, and trumpeters, shall be heard no more at all in thee; and the sound of a millstone shall be heard no more at all in thee; and the light of a candle shall shine no more at all in thee; and the voice of the bridegroom and of the bride shall be heard no more at all in thee: for thy merchants were the great men of the earth; for by thy sorceries were all nations deceived" (Rev. 18:10-13).

But—even in such a time of *great* tribulation, even during the very last period of degeneration, the true child of God must and shall stand firm! Mindful that the worldly city will *lose* all her culture and that the Christians will *inherit* it, the child of God will know even during the *final* holocaust: "Though an host should encamp against me, my heart shall not fear: though war should rise against me, in this will I be confident. One thing have I desired of the Lord, *that* will I seek after; that I may dwell in the house of the Lord all the days of my life, to behold the beauty of the Lord, and to enquire in His temple. For in the time of trouble He shall hide me in His pavilion: in the secret of His tabernacle shall He hide me; He shall set me upon a rock!" (Ps. 27:3-5). For Babylon the great shall fall, and be lost forever. But all its true culture shall be saved, and preserved forever, after the final judgment! For Babylon ultimately serves the New Jerusalem!—thus Schilder (cf. quotation in front of book).

* * * * *

Lastly, then, this brings us to a consideration of the role of culture particularly in the New Jerusalem on the new earth to come after the final judgment.

After the judgment, God will make all things new (Rev. 21:1-5). After the purging of this world by fire, there will be a renewed world in which righteousness shall dwell (I Pet. 3:7-13). The old things will have passed away, and sin shall be banished. When Jesus comes again, He shall bring the city of the New Jerusalem with Him. It will come down to the new earth from God out of heaven, adorned like a bride for her husband, and heaven and earth shall be united (Rev. 21:1-2). The joys of heaven shall be preserved, and expanded, as the saints receive back their bodies, albeit now glorified. For our new bodies, though glorified, will not be *essentially* different from our own present earthly bodies, any more than the new world to come will be *essentially* different from our present world—for the principle of continuity shall remain! It will be a *cleansed* world (I Cor. 7:31), but the *same* world as *this* world with all its fullness (Gen. 2:9; Prov. 11:30; Rev. 22:2)—for as the Psalmist faithfully prayed: "Let the *sinners* be *consumed* out of the earth" (Ps. 104: 35), and as Christ Himself has promised: "The *meek* . . . shall inherit *the earth*" (Matt. 5:5).

Yes, the Christian meek shall inherit the earth! Inherit the earth! The world and all its fulness! All trashy works of wood and hay and stubble shall be destroyed by fire, but all solid cultural works of gold and silver and precious stones shall remain (I Cor. 3:12-15). For all that is truly beautiful and lovely in this world's culture, shall be inherited and enjoyed by believers in the next. Yes, *true* culture is indestructible, and will be enjoyed by the covenant-keeping believers unto all eternity! The covenant-breaking non-Christian artists and scientists and musicians will indeed be lost eternally in hell, on account of the hardness of their hearts—but the work of their hands (insofar as it is true art, true science, and true music) will be saved for all eternity—and eternally enjoyed by God's own children on the new earth. For God, the Prime Author of all true culture, will never reject the work of His own hands! (Ps. 138:8).

For the new creation will include and even deepen the present totality of all cultural reality. Moreover, culture and nature will continue to unfold still further. For the new creation and the city of the New Jerusalem will continue to exist in the cosmic dimension of time—behold the *monthly* yield of the fruit of the tree of life (Rev. 22:2). The city will also have a numerical aspect—behold its twelve gates and angels and foundations (Rev. 21:12-14); a spatial aspect—behold its foursquare dimension of twelve thousand furlongs each (Rev. 21:16); a mechanical aspect—behold the movement of the kings of the earth into it (Rev. 21:24); a physical aspect—behold its precious stones and pearls and gold (Rev. 21:18-21); a botanical aspect—behold the fruit and the healing leaves of the tree of life (Rev. 22:2); and a psychical aspect—behold the wolf and the lamb feeding together, and the joyous feelings of all of the city's inhabitants (Isa. 65:25–66:22f.; Rev. 21:3-7).

Yet not only will nature be exalted, but man and his culture too. There will be a glorification: of logic, even in the analytical distinctions between the varieties of precious stones in the New Jerusalem (Rev. 21:19f.); of history, even in the glory and honor of the nations there (Rev. 21:24); of linguistics, even in the song of the redeemed, the song of Moses and the Lamb (Rev. 15:3); of sociology, even in the fact that saved kings will be servants of God (Rev. 21:24; 22:3); of economics, for God's elect shall long enjoy the work of their hands, and they shall build houses, and they shall plant vineyards (Isa. 65:21-22); of aesthetics, for eye hath not seen nor ear heard the things which God hath prepared for them that love Him (I Cor. 2:9); of law, for God's elect shall reign with Christ and sit every man under his (own) vine and under his (own) fig tree (Rev. 22:5; Mic. 4:4); and of ethics, in the life of the whole family of God, for love and charity never faileth (Eph. 3:24-15; I Cor. 13:8).

And faith? Faith is the substance of things hoped for, the evidence of things not seen (Heb. 11:1). Now we walk by faith, not by sight (II Cor. 5:7). Now we see through a glass darkly, but on the new earth we shall see face to face (I Cor. 13:12). There we shall have no temple, for the Lord God Almighty and the Lamb are the temple of it, and we shall see His face (Rev. 21:22; 22:4). And the whole cultural totality of this recreated reality will be sustained forever by the Triune Lord God Almighty, in Whom it will live and move and have its very being (Acts 17:28); for the city will have no need of the sun or the moon to shine in it, for the glory of God will lighten it, "and the Lamb is the light thereof" (Rev. 21:23).

Of this new Jerusalem, the holy city on the new earth, we read: "The kings of the earth do bring their glory and honor into it . . . , and they shall bring the glory and honor of the nations into it" (Rev. 21: 24, 26).

The glory and honor of the nations! The cultural treasures of all the peoples of the earth! The tremendous technology and commercial products of the United States; the music of Germany and Russia; the art of ancient Greece and Rome, of Spain and France, and of Holland and Italy; the exquisite gardens of Japan and of southwestern England; the breath-takingly beautiful carpets of Persia and Afghanistan; the folklore of the Afrikaners and the Irish; and the rock-paintings of the Bushmen! The music of Beethoven, Greig, and Rimsky-Korsakoff; the paintings of Rembrandt and Constable and da Vinci; the poetry of Goethe and Milton and Eugene Marais; the theology of Luther and Calvin and Augustine and Warfield—all cleansed from their present sinful accretions, and all exhibited and enjoyed and seen or heard in the halls and museums of the New Jerusalem, for all eternity! Enjoyed! For the meek shall inherit the earth.

But the people of God will not only inherit the earth and all its cultural treasures, its true art and true music now being composed by others, by both Christian and non-Christian artists and musicians alike. They will also enjoy the eternal fruits of their *own* earthly work—including their own cultural works—for "blessed are the dead which die in the Lord . . . , that they may rest from their labours; *and their works do follow them*" (Rev 14:13). On the new earth, the Christian artist will thus be able to view even his *own* paintings painted while still in this present world of ours, and the Christian architect will be able to survey (though perhaps on a smaller scale) his *own* buildings constructed during this present life, insofar as the work on earth of the artist and the architect was true art and true architecture, and after it has been *cleansed* from all its present imperfections—for "their *works* do follow them!" And thenceforth unto all eternity, month after month they will *continue* to employ their old cultural talents anew while also developing new skills and talents—to the glory of the Lord God of culture, and to the enjoyment of all of God's people. Hence, all works of true culture now being performed on this present earth—whether being executed by believer or unbeliever—have everlasting value, as implied in the Westminster Confession (chs. XVI & XXIII). Everything "good" which man does on earth, bears fruit for all eternity![33]

On the new earth, poetry will be immortalized in the new name written on each believer's own white stone, "which no man knoweth, saving he that receiveth it" (I Cor. 3:11-14; Rev. 2:17). Music will culminate in the new song sung by the "harpers harping with their harps," and in "the song of Moses, the servant of God, and the song of the Lamb" (Rev. 14:2; 15:3). Architecture will reach its consummate glory in the city of the New Jerusalem itself, the city built upon a great and high mountain, "the city which hath foundations, whose Builder and Maker is God" (Heb. 11:10). And what glorious foundations they shall be—a rainbow of dazzling colors, and a kaleidoscope of pleasing forms—massive foundations of multicolored precious stones! The great city itself, 1500 miles long and broad and high, will have the glory of God, and be illuminated by jasper-colored light. And it will be surrounded by a huge wall of jasper with twelve gates of pearl, through which gates the saved kings and nations (who apparently reside in the "suburban" or even in the "rural" areas of the new earth which surround the New Jerusalem) shall bring their honor and their glory, as they enter the city of God on top of the mountains (Isa. 2:2; Rev. 21: 10-18).

Geology will excel itself in the massive size and sheer beauty of the precious stones and precious metals. The earth will then have been turned inside-out, as it were, and the gold *now* so sparsely found deep inside the present earth, will *then* clothe the streets and buildings of the New Jerusalem. The entire city itself will be of pure gold, like transparent glass, and its foundations will be garnished with all kinds of multi-colored precious stones: jasper, sapphire, chalcedony, emerald, sardonyx, sardius, chrysolite, beryl, topaz, chrysoprasus, jacinth, and amethyst (Rev. 21:1, 8-21). Yes, the foundations of the holy city shall glisten like a rainbow—for God's covenant of works with Adam and God's rainbow covenant with Noah will then be fulfilled by the mighty rainbow-crowned Second Adam (I Cor. 15:22-47; Rev. 10:1-3) Who, seated upon God's rainbow throne (Rev. 4:3-11; 5:5-14), shall illuminate the city with the brightness of seven suns (Isa. 30:26; Rev. 21:23; 22:5).

Under such luminescence, photosynthesis in plants will reach its climax. Botany will reach its greatest glory in the plantations of the tree of life growing on both sides of the crystal river, and loaded down with its fruits every month. The desert shall rejoice, and blossom as the rose. It shall blossom abundantly, and rejoice even with joy and singing: the glory of Lebanon shall be given unto it, the excellency of Carmel and Sharon. The mountains and hills shall break forth into singing, and all the trees of the field shall clap their hands. Instead of the thorn, shall come up the fir tree; and instead of the brier, shall come up the myrtle tree.[33]

Zoology will culminate in the complete disappearance of enmity and the total restoration (or rather perfection!) of the Eden-like harmony among all living things. "The wolf . . . shall dwell with the lamb, and the leopard shall lie down with the kid, and the calf and the young lion and the fatling together; and a little child shall lead them. And the cow and the bear shall feed; their young ones shall lie down together; and the lion shall eat straw like the ox . . . and dust shall be the serpent's meat. . . ." However symbolic this language may be, and however much it admittedly at least partially refers to the present or future earthly reign of Christ, it also teaches the complete removal of the curse from the animal world as such in the everlasting state of the future too, when "they shall not hurt nor destroy in all My holy mountain," saith the Lord, "for the earth shall be full of the knowledge of the Lord, as the waters cover the sea!" (Isa. 11:6-9; 65:25).

The earth shall be full of the knowledge of the Lord! The new

---

33. Rev. 22:1-2; Isa. 35:1-2; 55:12-13; Micah 4:4; cf. Ezek. 47:12. Cf. too Matt. 5:5 and Rev. 14:13, and cf. our Third Appendix, below.

earth and all its fullness as the ultimate goal of culture—forever!

Thy will be done, O Father, here and now on earth, as it is being done here and now in heaven! And Thy will be done here and now on earth, as it will be done here on the renewed earth to come!

*   *   *   *   *

We summarize this chapter on the future fruits of culture.

First, we noted that all humanistic futurologists believe that man now has the power to control nature and to fashion the world he desires, but that—chiefly with the exception of the ultimately optimistic Marxists—there is increasing doubt as to the happy ending of our age, on account of the unhappy moral choices man may yet make as to the way in which to wield this power.

Second, it was seen that the Bible itself, however, in spite of all catastrophic occurrences in history, teaches an essential continuity in the cultural development from the past and through the present and into the future (and even beyond the grave). For God made the world in six days to be inhabited with plants and animals and men, preserving them down through the centuries and for life on the new earth to come. And the cultural works given to the first Adam, now unfold through the cultural works of the Second Adam, Whose post-resurrectional works are also a preview of our own post-resurrectional works inasmuch as we as children of the Second Adam will be like Him when He shall appear.

Third, we saw that the essential continuity between both nature and culture in this life and in the next has also been recognized by leading Christian thinkers down throughout Church history, especially in the West. Augustine, Jerome, and Thomas Aquinas among the pre-Reformational thinkers; Luther and Calvin in particular among the Reformers; and Abraham Kuyper, his sons H. H. Kuyper and Abraham Kuyper Jr., Bavinck, Dijk, and Berkouwer among the modern Reformed theologians—have all insisted that materiality is an essential aspect of the life to come.

Fourth, we saw that all of this is of the greatest practical importance. Correctly stressing the *material* and cultural nature of the future life here and now, not only guards against a false spiritual*istic*

91

misrepresentation of it (or an equally false material*istic* miscon-ception of it by way of reaction), but also makes our material and cultural work relevant to us here and now and even enables us to make Christianity more attractive to materially-interested or even materialistic unbelievers.

Fifth, it was seen that we are to work for the coming of the Kingdom here and now on earth as it is here and now in heaven, where Jesus is preparing a place for us and where the dead in Christ reign with and serve Him and are fed and clothed by Him and wor-ship Him while eagerly awaiting the coming of the Kingdom here on earth.

Sixth, this brought us to a consideration of the coming of the Kingdom here on earth between now and the time of Christ's second coming to unite heaven and earth. Here we saw that although He has in principle already set up His Kingdom here on earth, we our-selves through the power of His indwelling Spirit are to set it up everywhere in practice too, transforming the evil culture of this world more and more by the powerful proclamation of the life-transforming Gospel of Christ with all its cultural implications, until history reaches its consummation when Jesus comes again.

Then, lastly, we saw how Jesus will bring the heavenly city with Him down to earth, purify the earth with fire, transforming it unto the everlasting dwelling place of His people, who will thenceforth not only enjoy all the true and then purified culture which they and others ever produced previously when on our present earth, but which culture they will also continue to produce on the new earth as they thenceforth too continue to glorify God and enjoy Him forever![34]

* * * * *

What then can we learn from all the above? How should this revealed knowledge of the future affect our lives here and now?

First, we should understand that the life to come will not only perfect but also *purify* our present life and all its culture, without

---

34. *Westminster Shorter Catechism*, Q. 1.

discounting its permanent importance and everlasting abiding significance. When God's Word tells us that Abraham and the patriarchs were "strangers and pilgrims on the earth" (Heb. 11:13 cf. Gen. 47:9), although they were obviously grieved by the *sinfulness* in the world as they passed through it, they were in no way ill at ease on account of the *earthiness* of the world as such.[35] To the contrary, rather did they regard the earthly Canaan as the *hallway* to the inner sanctuary of the heavenly Canaan (Gen. 17:6-8; Rev. 21:2, 24-26); and somehow they knew that the heavenly city they were seeking would ultimately be established *here on our ultimately purified earth* (Heb. 11:14-16, 9-10, 22; Gen. 49:29; 50:24f.). After all, even the *unfallen Adam* was a *stranger* in Eden (having been created *outside* of the garden—Gen. 2:8), and was destined to *leave* that garden (Gen. 2:24) on his *pilgrimage* through the world as he *"lived"* and multiplied and filled or *replenished the whole earth* (Gen. 1:28) on his probational journey from losable everlasting life to unlosable everlasting life (Gen. 2:17)! And as the Belgic Confession insists: "We believe, according to the Word of God, . . . that our Lord Jesus Christ will come from heaven, . . . burning this old world with fire and flame to *cleanse* it."[36] May we too then believe that our present world is not to be annihilated, but to be purified. And may we act accordingly and value and improve it!

Second, we can hardly close our eyes to the *continuity* between this life and the next, and therefore to the continuity between the culture of this life and the culture of the next. Accordingly, we should together with the Second Helvetic Confession "therefore condemn all who deny a *real resurrection* of the *flesh* (II Tim. 2:18), or who with John of Jerusalem, against whom Jerome wrote, do not have a correct view of the glorification of *bodies*."[37] And together with the Westminster Confession of Faith, we too should believe that "after death . . . the souls of the righteous, being then

---

35. Van der Waal, *Wat staat er eigenlijk?* (Goes, Netherlands: Oosterbaan & Le Cointre, 1971), pp. 172-175.

36. Art. 37. KJV's "burned up" at II Pet. 3:10 should read "found"! Cf. too Matt. 13:29-30, 39-43, 49-50 & I Cor. 3:10-14.

37. *Second Helvetic Confession*, chap. XI.

made perfect in holiness, are received into the highest heavens, where they behold the face of God in light and glory, *waiting for the full redemption of their bodies,"* and that "at the last day, . . . all *the dead shall be raised up with the selfsame bodies, and none other,* although with different qualities, which shall be united *again* to their souls *for* ever."[38]

And if our bodies are *then* to remain with our souls for all eternity, we should surely treasure them *now* too—together with all the true cultural works they are now producing! (I Cor. 6:19f.). For as the Heidelberg Catechism (Q. 1) reminds us, my "only comfort *in life and in death"* is that "I, with *body* and soul, both in *life* and *death,* am not my own, but belong unto my faithful Savior Jesus Christ; Who . . . by His Holy Spirit assures me of everlasting life, and makes me heartily *willing* and ready *henceforth* (!) to live unto Him!"

Lastly, we can surely learn that all that we are doing here and now of any value, will not only have permanent consequences but is itself *permanent* and will endure for ever (after purification) on the new earth to come. As *Abraham Kuyper* said, Revelation 21: 24-26 ("and the kings of the earth . . . shall bring their glory and honour of the nations into it" [that is, into the city of the New Jerusalem on the new earth to come]) teaches us that "the continuing societal development which has been and which still will be reached in the history of nations" will "be exhibited as the *permanent new condition"* on the "new earth and under the new heaven, after the final judgment."[39] For then, as the Westminster Larger Catechism assures us, God's elect will experience "the *full* redemption of their *bodies"* and shall be *"filled* with inconceivable *joys,* made perfectly holy and *happy* both in *body* and soul, . . . especially in the immediate vision and *fruition* of God the Father, of our Lord Jesus Christ, and of the Holy Spirit, *to all* eternity."[40] Accordingly, since no cultural work of value we perform here and now will ever

---

38. *Westminster Confession of Faith,* 32:1-2.
39. Kuyper, *Van de Voleinding,* I, 463-464.
40. *Westminster Larger Catechism,* Q. 86, 90.

94

be lost, "therefore, my beloved brethren, be stedfast, unmoveable, *always abounding in the work of the Lord,* forasmuch as ye know that *your labour is not in vain* in the Lord!" (I Cor. 15:58).

* * * * *

"O Lord, how great are Thy works!" (Ps. 92:6). "How precious are Thy thoughts unto me, O God! How great is the sum of them! If I should count them, they are more in number than the sand!" (Ps. 139:17-18). "Eye hath not seen, nor ear heard, neither have entered into the heart of man, the things which God hath prepared for them that love Him!" (I Cor. 2:9).

"O the depth of the riches, both of the wisdom and the knowledge of God! . . . For *of* Him, and *through* Him, and *to* Him, are *all* things: to Whom be glory for ever!" (Rom. 11:33, 36).

V

THE HARVESTING OF CULTURE

When Adolf Hitler first started his mighty *Kulturkampf* or Cultural Struggle and called for a specifically German cultural approach to art and science and technology in order to build his millennial *Deutsches Reich* or thousand-year German Empire,[1] the rest of the world softly sniggered. One decade later, as Europe lay smoldering in ruins, the world sniggered no longer. For ideas, and especially seemingly crackpot cultural ideas, *do* have consequences.

When equally crackpot nineteenth-century evolutionists first suggested that man had come up from ape-like ancestors, the incredulous Victorian establishment sniggered. However, when the state appellate court in 1927 reversed the decision of the famous John T. Scopes trial, thereby allowing the Tennessee school teacher to advocate evolution in the public schoolroom,[2] the sniggering quieted down a little. And today, as evolutionism reigns paramount in the public education system from coast to coast, we snigger no longer. For evolutionism has in fact now become the new establishment, and is now deeply entrenched in the life of the nation's schools, universities, courts, hospitals, congresses—and churches. So deeply: that supposedly once broad-minded liberal educationalists have now "evolved" into biased bigots, who have cynically banished the Bible from the public schools; that juridical retribution has now "evolved" into "social rehabilitation"; that the legitimate interests of this one nation under God have "evolved" into the illegitimate interests of no God over the United Nations; that hospitals are fast "evolving"

---

1. Cf. Adolf Hitler, *My Struggle* (London: Paternoster Press, 1936).
2. Cf. *Encyclopedia Americana*, 1952 ed., art., "Scopes."

from sanatoriums for the sick into abattoirs of abortion (and, perhaps very soon, into slaughterhouses for senior citizens); and even many churches have already "evolved" from temples of the living God into synagogues of Satan. Truly, ideas *do* have consequences!

Yet again, when the crackpot communists Marx and Engels drew up their *Communist Manifesto,* calling for the abolition of landed property, a heavy graduated income tax, centralization of credit and of the means of communication and transport in the hands of the state, and free education of all children in public schools,[3] the world once again sniggered. However, after the Red takeover of Russia, when Lenin published his *Communist Organization and Strategy,* alias his *Twenty-One Conditions for World Takeover,* calling for systematic propaganda and agitation, support for movements of liberation in the colonies, persistent work in the labor unions, and the waging of a decisive war against the entire bourgeois world,[4] the sniggering subsided. And today, with the Soviet Union currently in what many Western observers regard as a position of apparently increasing overall military superiority,[5] and with Red China after its "Cultural Revolution" now stepping up its considerable nuclear armory and delivery system, our sniggering has ceased altogether. For when cultured Russian ballet-lovers and chess-players and cultured Chinese tea-drinkers and pingpong-players start rattling their nuclear toys instead of their chessmen and their pingpong balls, and while the hammer and sickle extend their menacing shadows more and more over the face of the earth, culture-conscious Christians had better reach for their Biblical sickle and hammer out a Christian counter-offensive in order to reap the world's cultural fruits—before the communists do.

Fellow Christian! God's Word is "like a hammer that breaketh the rock," like a hammer that breaks open even the stoniest and toughest

---

3. Marx and Engels, *Manifesto of the Communist Party* (Moscow: Progress Publishers, n.d.), pp. 90-91.
4. Lenin, *Communist Organization and Strategy,* in *Blueprints for World Conquest as Outlined by the Communist International* (Washington: U.S. Government Printing Office, 1946), pp. 65-72.
5. Cf. Lee, *Communist Eschatology,* pp. 947-955.

resistance to the acknowledgement of our Saviour's Lordship! (cf. Jer. 23:29). So then, "thrust in *thy* sickle and reap! For the time is come for thee to reap! For the harvest of the earth is *ripe!*" (Rev. 14:15).

* * * * *

In this final chapter, then, we shall seek to develop a Christian plan to harvest the world's culture. First, we must see that we dare not ignore the cultural challenge. Second, we must appreciate that we are no longer living in the Edenic period of culture and can never go back to it or to any other previous period—nor should we try to do so. Third, we must preserve all that is "good" in fallen man's culture. Fourth, we must cleanse that which is bad but which is still utilizable in our culture. Fifth, we must unequivocally reject all that is unchristianizable in our culture. And sixth, we must implement a specifically Biblical Christian cultural program.

* * * * *

First, then, we must see that we dare not ignore the cultural challenge. Surely we have realized by now that the evolutionists and the communists just as much mean business in their attempts to gain control of the cultural formative powers throughout the world as did Hitler in his furious onslaught against Western civilization. But more importantly, we should even more deeply realize that the Bible *even more* means business when it calls for a Christian cultural crusade.

Let us then briefly review our Biblical findings, and see how God's Word insists that we may no longer ignore the call to develop a Christian approach to culture, but are to get involved, for Jesus' sake!

We have heretofore been comparing culture to a plant, and have discussed its roots, its growth, its blossoming, and its fruits; in this last chapter we shall discuss its harvesting.

In our first chapter, on the *roots* of culture, we saw that the Bible itself stresses the God-*grounded* and God-*centered* character of all true culture. For God not only created the raw materials of nature which man turns into culture, but God also sustains them all, so that it is only in God that we live and move and have our very being (Acts 17:28). We also saw that human culture should dominate the whole earth and sea and sky under God's guidance and to God's glory. And we also saw that life without a cultural commitment is meaningless even to modern man, inasmuch as God's covenant of works with Adam involves all men down through all the ages in cultural activity, for which they shall be judged on the coming Day of the Lord after the conclusion of God's seventh day, which is co-extensive with human history.

In our second chapter, on the *growth* of culture, we saw that even after the fall, God Himself immediately guaranteed the further development of culture by promising (in the prophecy of the coming Seed of the woman) to incarnate Himself as the Second Adam. Between the fall and the flood, we saw that culture developed particularly strongly in the line of Cain, and after the flood we saw how God's universal covenant with Noah provided all the essential preconditions for the continued development of culture. Further, we saw how the God-ordained events at the tower of Babel promoted the unfolding of culture, particularly in its multinational pluriformity. We next analyzed the theocratic culture of Old Testament Israel, and finally we saw how all the great old-world cultures more and more focused on the land of Israel in post-exilic times.

In chapter three, on the *blossoming* of culture, we saw that the cultural crisis of the world at the time of the human birth of Jesus Christ cried out for the advent of such a Leader to redirect its cultural development. We saw that culture did indeed blossom in the earthly life of Jesus, and that His resurrection and ascension into heaven and His session as the Second Adam on the throne of the universe represented His human assumption of all cultural power over the entire universe. His subsequent outpouring of His all-enabling Spirit into the Christian Church as His earthly people, we saw, renewed the dynamic development of true culture. And even though some Christians like Clement and Origen uncritically absorbed the influences of heathen culture, and others like Tertullian impoverished Christianity by declaring war against all culture as such, the balanced position represented by Augustine ultimately prevailed, and, especially after the Reformation, particularly

99

in Calvin and the Calvinists do we see the further blossoming of culture in the deliberate attempts made to Christianize it, thus bringing untold blessings to men and women everywhere.

In chapter four, on the *fruits* of culture, we saw that the basic doctrinal teachings of the Bible indicate an essential continuity in the cultural development from the past through the present and into the future, for God has never abandoned His creation, the work of His own hands, and continues to unfold it even today. Furthermore, we saw that leading Christian thinkers in all ages of Church history have recognized this to be the teaching of the Bible, and that our recognizing here and now the cultural nature of the life to come is invaluable in giving meaning to our careers and labors in our present lives as a preparation for the next life. For even now in heaven, the departed saints are glorifying the God of culture in their many activities there, and after the final judgment, when the heavenly city of the New Jerusalem comes down to the renewed earth, all the inherited benefits of the good culture of this present world, then purified, will be enjoyed and further developed forever.

From every perspective, then, we *dare* not ignore the cultural challenge today, but we must go in and harvest it for God!

* * * * *

Second, we must, however, understand that there can be no return to the culture of the garden of Eden or to that of any other period of the past, as we set about our present attempt at Christian cultural reconstruction.

Just as each subsequent day of God's formation week carried the world forward to a further stage of development than had been realized on the preceding day(s), and just as during that time there was never an annihilation of our once-and-for-all created world and never once a fresh creation of a brand new world all over again from the beginning (even though there were subsequent purges of man's sinful condition though without ever annihilating his world!), so too will there never be a return to the cultural level of Eden—even though the cultural institutions of Eden such as marriage and labor and the sabbath have, of course, all come down to us nonetheless.

Indeed, even an *attempt* to return to Eden would prove impossible of realization. For in Eden there were only two people in the world, whereas today there are around four billion. Then men were sinless and naked; today even Christians are sinners, and wear clothes like the rest of mankind. Then there was not yet any heavy industry; today tractors and factories and jetliners pollute the erstwhile silence of the air.

Moreover, man was never intended to remain on the same cultural level at which he was originally created. He was destined agri-culturally to multiply the one tree of life in Eden into the whole groves of the tree of life that will one day grow on the new earth (Gen. 2:9; Rev. 22:2). He was intended to leave Eden and to fill the earth with his descendants (Gen. 1:28; 2:24), which is what we should do, rather than to try to relocate back in Eden. He was to design and develop clothes and wear them, as Jesus the Second Adam did and still does, and as we too should do, rather than anachronistically and indeed anti-culturally try to establish "Christian"(?!) nudist colonies. And Adam was to multiply and to diversify the human race—which is what we too should do, rather than to attempt to straitjacket our individual personalities into the stereotyped mold of one-world socialistic man.

Again, even though the Paradise of the future will be sinless (as was Eden), unlike Eden it will also incorporate the positive cultural gains developed *since* the fall, at least some of which could hardly have come into being had the fall never occurred. Only after the flood (as God's punishment for sin) was the beautiful rainbow given under the universal Noachic covenant (Gen. 2:5; 9:12-17); yet the rainbow is incorporated into our future life in heaven (Rev. 4:1-3; 10:1). Only after the exodus from the bondage of Egypt were the names of the twelve tribes of Israel engraved into the precious stones on the breastplate of the high priest of Israel (Ex. 28:9-21); yet their names shall also be written forever on the precious stone foundations and on the gates of the New Jerusalem on the new earth to come (Rev. 21:10-21). There was no man Christ Jesus in Eden; only the eternal Son of God. Yet, as a result of the Son's incarnation and His unique human obedience to the

Adamitic covenant of works (Heb. 2:5-17), on the new earth to come the blessings of His incarnation and its fruits will endure forever (Rev. 21:22-23). Hence, any repristination or even any attempt to return to Eden would therefore represent not only a cultural impoverishment and retrogression from our present stage of cultural development thus far achieved, but also a denial of the reality of history!

Similarly, there can be no return to any other once-and-for-all historical events—such as the creation of the universe and of man by God the Father, such as the human birth and Calvary death of Jesus Christ, or such as the inauguration of the New Testament Church by the outpouring of the gift of God the Holy Spirit. All of theses events, and of similar once-and-for-all occurrences such as natural and cultural miracles, all of which had profound cultural implications, just do not bear imitative repetition (Heb. 2:4; 10:10). So too, there can be no return to the cultural *level* of Israel in the wilderness under the Mosaic covenant, no return to the cultural *milieu* of the Christian community in the first-century Jerusalem, and not even a return to the pre-industrial Geneva of John Calvin—*even though, of course, we are to extract the permanent Christian cultural principles from all of these situations,* and, under the guidance of God's Holy Spirit, apply them faithfully to our own different situation in twentieth-century America.

*　　*　　*　　*　　*

Third, realizing that there is much in fallen man's cultural development which has permanent value, we should endeavor to preserve and "harvest" it, for the Bible tells us to "prove [or test] *all* things; [and to] *hold fast* to that which is *good"* (I Thess. 5:21). And that at least *some* of the things produced even by fallen man are worth preserving for the future, is the unanimous view of representative leaders of all the various leading schools of Christian eschatology.

The premillennialistic scholar, J. Oliver Buswell Jr., for example, believed that "man was intended *and is destined* to have dominion over all the earth and all the creatures upon it . . . The command to rule the earth, given before man became a sinner (Gen. 1:26ff.), was repeated to Noah and his posterity, after the devastation of the flood (Gen. 8:15–9:17), after mankind had become a sinful race"; and Buswell further believed that "God's image in man, which is related to man's intended rule over the earth," should be regarded "as a key for interpretation of the entire biblical doctrine of human culture,"[6] which human culture embraces history, physical and cultural anthropology, morality, the family, the state, economics, and the church.[7]

The South African amillennialistic scholar Kees van der Waal is also stimulating when he approves of Schilder's statement that "gasoline rather than incense is an *explicit* theme of the Bible,"[8] and then goes on to add himself: "Nothing is absolutized here, for here there is only fear and trembling before the God Who tells me: 'What God hath joined together (prayer and exploitation), let no man put asunder!' And again: 'What God hath cleansed, that call not thou common!' . . . Let us beware lest texts and terms wrenched out of their context may bring us to the false dilemma: Christ *or* culture. On the *pietist's* road of the pilgrim's progress to eternity, the cultural mandate dies, and we no longer know how to do anything meaningful with our riches—and then we stand not knowing what to say (*met een mond vol tanden*) before today's challenging problems. I shall never forget a conversation with an old nurseryman about pot-plants. We were discussing the point made about the 'cultural mandate' by Dr. Douma in his dissertation[9]—which he (the nurseryman!) had read three times. Do we only have a *modest* cultural task? Are we *only* strangers and pilgrims here on earth? The nurseryman said: 'I am more than seventy-five years old, and really don't need to work any more. Did you think'—and here his hand executed a broad sweep over the beautiful bromelias, begonias, delicious monsters, and other

---

6. Buswell, *A Systematic Theology of the Christian Religion* (Grand Rapids: Zondervan, 1962), I, 344-345.
7. *Ibid.*, pp. 341-429.
8. Schilder, in, *De Reformatie* (Goes, Netherlands, March 27, 1936); cf. in Puchinger, *Een Theologie in Discussie* (Kampen: J. H. Kok, 1970).
9. Douma, *Algemene Genade* [that is, *Common Grace*] (Goes, Netherlands: Oosterbaan & Le Cointre, 1966).

treasures in the large greenhouse—'Did you think I only work to eat? I do it to glorify my Creator!' "[10]

And the American postmillennialistic scholar Loraine Boettner also significantly states: "We look upon science, education, invention, art, music, commerce, statesmanship, sociology, etc., each in its own field so far as it is based on truth, as a revelation of the wisdom and glory of Christ, Who is the Light of the world and the Ruler of the nations. Each of these represents an accomplishment in man's conquest of the forces of nature, which was the task assigned to him when immediately after his creation he was commanded to 'subdue' the earth; and each of these is a prophecy of the complete establishment of Christ's Kingdom. . . . Up to the present time we have had only a foretaste of this great Golden Age, and that in very limited communities. But we see the forces of righteousness advancing, and the forces of evil in retreat; and we look forward to the time when the Gospel shall have won its complete victory and when (as a result of man's increased diligence and his advanced knowledge in the realms of agriculture, biology, chemistry, engineering, etc.) even nature shall reflect gloriously the change that has occurred in the hearts of men,—'when the wilderness and the dry land shall be glad; and the desert shall rejoice and blossom as the rose,' Is. 35:1. . . . If this reasoning is correct, the human race may yet be in its infancy, with a future course of development in store which may well be utterly beyond the power of our imagination to grasp. In the physical realm we are now only on the threshold of the age of electronics, atomic power, and space travel; and who can predict what limitless fields of expansion and conquest both on the earth and throughout the universe these may open up! Dr. Warfield used to say that we still are in the Primitive Church, and that doctrinally the so-called 'church fathers' might better have been called the 'church infants.' In any event, we may be sure that as God's plan for the Church and for the development of His Kingdom at large is revealed to us, it will be, like His other works, incredibly greater in time and scope

---

10. Van der Waal, *Het Cultuurmandaat in Discussie* (Pretoria, South Africa: Servire, Villieria, 1971), pp. 37-38.

than our little minds can grasp. At the time of man's creation one of the commands given to him was that he should 'subdue' the earth (Gen. 1:28-30)—that is, search out the laws of nature, learn to apply them for his own advancement, and so make himself master of all animate and inanimate things which have been placed here for his use. He still is a long way behind on that schedule. But beyond all that, God's work of bringing new souls, infinitely precious souls, into the Kingdom, is a continuing work of the utmost importance. How thankful we should be that He did not terminate that work before our time! . . . Let us ever remember that Christ is our King here and now, that He is ruling and overruling through the whole course of human history, making the wrath of men to praise Him, and able even to bring good out of that which men intend for evil."[11]

From all the various eschatological perspectives, then, as seen above, man *ought* to be involved in preserving his cultural heritage and in promoting further cultural activities. It is true, as the Inter-Varsity Press writer Triton points out,[12] that "the Christian attitude to culture has often been ambiguous," but as Triton also points out: "At the very beginning of the world, however, man was given a mandate to subdue the earth (Gen. 1:28). . . . Sin has made the task doubly important (and also relatively distasteful), but it has not altered the basic mandate to control nature and use it for our good. Mankind has a God-appointed task, therefore, to make an increasingly good use of the resources of nature, and the Christian of all people should be foremost in aiming at progress in this realm. . . . The tasks of advancing knowledge and of subduing the earth have been enthusiastically pursued by Christians all down the ages, if their thinking has been truly biblical. The Christian should believe in this sense in progress and aim to contribute to it."[13]

As Hepp once declared: "Through His common grace, God has

---

11. Lorraine Boettner, *Studies in Theology* (Grand Rapids: Eerdmans, 1957), pp. 253-254; and cf. too his, *The Millennium* (Philadelphia: Presbyterian and Reformed Publishing Co., 1972), pp. 348-349.

12. Triton, *Whose World?—The Christian's Attitude to the Material World, to Culture, Politics, Technology, Society* . . . (London: Inter-Varsity Press, 1970), p. 47.

13. *Ibid.*, pp. 44-45.

taken care that science falsely so-called (*de pseudo-wetenschap*) has *not* rebelled against *all* aprioric revealed truths. It accepts *some* of them. To this extent, it possesses fragments of true knowledge."[14] And as Van Peursen remarks: "The Christian should recognize God's activity in non-Christian thought,"[15] which is not, of course, to say that all or even most non-Christian thought meets with God's approval, but which is to say that God does *sometimes* act in revealing some of His truths in some of the thoughts of non-Christians. And, as Hepp concluded, the true knowledge of Christian thinkers, according to divine decree, *does* need (the fruits) of "science falsely so-called"[16]—although such does, of course, always first need re-interpreting in terms of the Bible.

For, as Calvin stated, he who ignores the true insights of philosophers like Plato and physicians like Galen, insults not *them* but *God the Holy Spirit* Who gave them their many true insights even in spite of their own total depravity![17] And, as Isaiah remarked, at sowing time it is *God* Who instructs the plowman to break the clods of his ground and to cast abroad the fitches and scatter the cummin and cast in the principal wheat and the appointed barley and the rye in their place (Isa. 28:24-26). And at harvest time, the fitches are not threshed, neither is the cummin cartwheeled, but beaten out, and bread corn is bruised and not crushed by the reaper's horses—*because this knowledge too "cometh forth from the Lord of hosts, Which is wonderful in counsel, and excellent in working!"* (Isa. 28:27-29).

So, then, as Grosheide concludes, "he who withdraws himself [from cultural involvement], does not allow the Word of God to resound over [all of] life, but does allow the world to remain without God! It is the constant task of the Christian to evaluate culture according to the Word of God, to influence culture from the Word of God, to lead culture further according to the Word of God, and yet

---

14. Hepp, *De Basis van de eenheid der wetenschap* (Netherlands, 1937).
15. Van Peursen, *Filosofische Orientatie* (Kampen, 1958), p. 135.
16. Cf. Wielenga, *op. cit.*, p. 265, n. 8.
17. Calvin, *Institutes of the Christian Religion*, I:5:2; I:15:16; II:2:15; II:3:3-4.

to guard himself against being dragged along by the forces opposed to God which are operative within culture."[18]

*   *   *   *   *

Fourth, then, we must cleanse that which is bad, but which is still utilizable, in our culture.

We Christians should not avoid our culture, as did Tertullian and the later pietists, nor uncritically absorb it all, as did Clement and Origen, but we should cleanse and use all utilizable aspects of our modern cultural heritage, as did Augustine and particularly Calvin and the later Calvinists.

Let us note how Noah "inherited" and utilized all the antediluvian cultural achievements in agriculture and music and engineering which he borrowed from the ungodly Cainites to build his ark and plant his vineyard.[19] Also, it is instructive to note how the Priest-King Melchizedek—a type of Jesus Christ, the Second Adam! (Heb. 6: 20-26)—was enriched by Abraham's tithes obtained from goods which he had derived from the godless king of Sodom (Gen. 14:11-22 cf. chs. 18–19). So too, Jacob acquired great herds derived from the off-spring of the deceitful Laban's flocks (Gen. chs. 30–31); and his son Joseph gained control over much of the land of the heathen Egyptians (Gen. chs. 41 and 47).

Moreover, Moses acquired much wisdom, both from the Egyptians (Heb. 11:26) and from Jethro the Midianite (Ex. chs. 2–4 and 18), all of which wisdom stood him in good stead to lead his people out of Egypt and through the wilderness. And when they left their Egyptian oppressors, the Israelites "borrowed" their jewels and silver and gold (Ex. 3:21-22), all of which—after the brief misuses of the gold in the making of the golden calf! (Ex. 32)—were re-utilized again (and this time in a godly way!) to build the tabernacle and its furnishings (Ex. 35:5f.), even as Eleazar the priest made the brazen censers of the wicked company of Korah into broadplates as a covering of the altar (Num. 16:39). Similarly, Joshua took possession of the land

---

18. *Op. cit.*, pp. 527-528.
19. Gen. 4:20-22 cf. 6:14-16; I Pet. 3:20; II Pet. 2:5; Gen. 9:20.

of Canaan from the heathen and put it to better use for the benefit of the people of God (Josh. chs. 6–22); Solomon utilized the cedars of Lebanon with which to build the temple of the Lord (I Kings 5:8-10); and even the hire and merchandise of the fornicating Tyre of old was to become "holiness to the Lord" for the benefit of "them that dwell before the Lord!" (Isa. 23:18).

Prophetically, in the future, *even more* such cultural riches are to accrue to the benefit of God's elect—even here and now in *this* world of ours *this* side of the final judgment. The Assyrians and the Egyptians and the Ethiopians and other nations and all their riches shall come into the Christian Church,[20] and the wilderness and the desert shall rejoice and blossom as the rose (Isa. 35). For thus saith the Lord God of culture to His people here on earth: "I will give thee the treasures of darkness . . . and hidden riches of secret places. . . . The labor of Egypt, and merchandise of Ethiopia and of the Sabeans, men of stature, shall come over unto thee, and they shall be thine" (Isa. 45:3, 14). Zion or the Christian Church shall yet put on her beautiful garments (Isa. 52:1f.), and she shall inherit the Gentiles and all their riches (Isa. 54:3, 11f.). The abundance of the sea and the forces of the Gentiles shall accrue to her— gold and incense and flocks and silver and precious woods and iron and glory (Isa. 60:3-21; cf. chs. 62 and 66). And God's New Testament people shall (re)build waste cities and inhabit them, and plant vineyards and drink the wine thereof, and make gardens and eat the fruit of them (Amos 9:11-14 cf. Acts 15:15-17).

As Hugh Black remarked: "The birthplace of modern civilization is not Athens, but Calvary. The 'pale Galilean' has conquered against all the full-blooded gospels of the natural joy of life, but conquered in the grandest way of conquest, not by the extermination of the opponent, but by changing the enemy into a friend. When the sons of Greece are not against but for the sons of Zion (cf. Zech. 9:13); when all ideals of culture find their inspiration and nourishment in the divine ideals of Jesus, and take their place in the great loving world-purpose of the world's Saviour; when thought,

---

20. Isa. 11:10-16; 27:12-13 cf. 45:14.

and art, and literature, and knowledge, and life are brought into subjection to the obedience of Christ, *that* is the true victory!" And as Bavinck has told us: "It behooves the Christians to enrich their temple with the vessels of the Egyptians and to adorn the crown of Christ, their King, with the pearls brought up from the sea of paganism. . . . Hence the believer cannot rest contented in his faith, but must make it the point of vantage from which he mounts up to the source of election and presses forward to the conquest of the entire world."[21]

The whole of world history, then, is ultimately subservient to the history of the people of God![22] Truly, God's meek children are blessed indeed! And the blessed meek shall yet inherit the earth! (Matt. 5:5).

*   *   *   *   *

Fifth, however, our Biblical evaluation of our culture will sometimes lead us to *reject* some of its aspects, as Grosheide implicitly suggests.[23] For God's Word, after telling us to *prove* (or test) all things, and to *hold fast* that which is *good,* immediately goes on to declare: *"Abstain* from all the appearance of *evil"* (I Thess. 5: 21-22). Indeed, the *antithesis* between *Christian culture* and *worldly culture* must *inescapably be emphasized.*

Now it should hardly be necessary to say that it is precisely the *Ten Commandments* which God's Word constantly[24] refers us to as the standard for determining good from evil even today, as we have pointed out in detail elsewhere.[25] The real problem arises, however, in applying the Ten Commandments in practice to evaluate the Chris-

---

21. Black, *op. cit.,* p. 383; cf. Bavinck, "Calvin and Common Grace," in *The Princeton Theological Review* (Princeton, N. J.: Princeton University Press, 1909), no. 3, pp. 441, 462.

22. Grosheide, *De brief van Paulus aan de Efeziërs* (Kampen, 1960), p. 89; cf. Eph. 1:4-23; 5:22-32 cf. Gen. 1:26-28 & Deut. 32:8 & Rev. 21:21-26.

23. Grosheide, *Cultuur,* pp. 527-528.

24. Ex. 20; Isa. 8:20; Mal. 4:4; Matt. 5:17-19; 19:17-19; Rom. 2:12-22; 3:31; 7:7, 12, 14, 21-22; 13:9; Eph. 6:1-4; James 2:8-11; I John 3:4; Rev. 12:17.

25. Lee, "Are the Ten Commandments Still Applicable Today?", in *Blue Banner* (Beaver Falls, Pa.), 1st quarter, 1974.

tian's attitude to such questionable cultural phenomena as, for example: risky investment opportunities, Sunday newspapers, methods of birth control, professional sport, card games, trade with communist Cuba, state charity lotteries, ballroom dancing lessons, and the cultivation and marketing of tobacco. What should our attitude be toward these aspects of our culture?

In the last analysis, each must make his own decision *coram Deo,* or alone before the Lord (cf. Rom. 14:2-12, 22-23). But this decision must be made with an *enlightened* understanding and a sensitive *conscience,* thoroughly *exposed* to the searchlight of the Ten Commandments and motivated by a deep love of God and a tender concern for one's fellow man. And living as we do in an age when the national conscience has been blunted (as evidenced by the widescale use of dangerous drugs and the legalization of abortions and the widescale breakdown of political morality), it would certainly be advisable to consider some of the phenomena which the well-tested Westminster Larger Catechism regards as belonging to the *appearance* of evil and which are therefore to be avoided by the Christian, namely: atheism, idolatry, heresy, black magic, and fortune-telling (Q. 105); depicting God or adding to the principles of Biblical liturgical culture (Q. 109); profane jokes, vain janglings, and charms (Q. 113); unnecessary idleness from godly meditation and needless thoughts about our worldly employments and recreations on the sabbath (Q. 119); neglect of employmental duties and inordinate seeking of ease or profit or pleasure (Q. 128-130); withdrawing of the necessary means of preservation of life (cf. euthanasia!) and immoderate use of meat, drink, labor, and recreations (Q. 136); sodomy, filthy communications, immodest apparel, tolerating brothels, unjust divorce, lascivious songs, books, pictures, dancings, and stage plays (Q. 139); fraud, false weights and measures, removing landmarks (cf. international border disputes!), unfaithfulness in contracts, engrossing commodities to enhance the price, unlawful callings, inordinate prizing and affecting of worldly goods, idleness, prodigality, wasteful gaming, and defrauding ourselves of the due use and comfort of that estate which God hath given us (Q. 142); holding our peace when iniquity calleth for either a reproof from

110

ourselves or complaint to others, or speaking the truth unseasonably, or maliciously to a wrong end, or thinking or speaking too lightly or too meanly of ourselves or others (Q. 145); and discontentment with our own estate, and envying and grieving at the good(s) of our neighbor (Q. 147).

In addition, even though we are encouraged to enjoy all things which God has created (I Tim. 4:1-5) and to allow no man to rob us of the Christ-bought freedom of enjoying them (Gal. 5:1f. and cf. n. 20), *we should nevertheless avoid utilizing cultural phenomena not in themselves wrong* (such as meat previously dedicated to idols, or fermented wine) *in those circumstances where our use of them will probably cause weaker brethren to stumble* (Rom. 14:14-21; I Cor. 8:4-13).

Yet even our concern for our weaker *brother* (as opposed to our unbelieving *neighbor*) may never persuade us *always* to avoid the enjoyment and promotion of cultural phenomena. Still less should we allow the *unbeliever's* attitude toward our use of these things or not to influence our decisions appreciably. "For the earth is the *Lord's,* and the fullness thereof" (Ps. 24:1); so that the unbeliever, in the last analysis, is a trespasser on God's private property, and should not be allowed to dictate to the legitimate heirs how the latter should use that property. After all, trespassers should be prosecuted—not accommodated!

* * * * *

Sixth, however, cultural victory in this world here and now will not come to us if we merely sit back and fold our hands. As in salvation, we ourselves must work out our own program for cultural victory with fear and trembling—while (of course!) recognizing that it is *God* Who works in us both to will and to do of His own good pleasure! (cf. Phil. 2:12-13). And we must not only stand against the stream of today's largely unbelieving culture, but we must wade up to its source, and redivert its flow *away* from its apostasy and *back* to God! For as Grosheide writes, the Christian must not only attempt to check the dechristianization of culture, but he must also try to create his own sphere of influence in which God's Word is dominant—a style of life which will accept the treasures of culture, but which, after first testing them, will again attempt to bring to life whatever the Scriptures demand.[26]

Fortunately, quite a bit of work has already been done in pioneering the clear articulation of a Christian approach to culture.

Abraham Kuyper—best known in the United States for his short *Stone Lectures* on Calvinism and culture,[27] after first writing his monumental three-volume appreciation of the worthwhile cultural products of the unregenerate (entitled *Common Grace*),[28] next wrote his equally monumental three-volume plea to culturally gifted Christians to promote a specifically Christian culture (entitled *For the King*),[29] as well as his equally monumental practical plan to move toward specifically political Christian control (as embodied in his *Our Program*[30] and his *Antirevolutionary Statecraft*[31]). And, in addition to cultural ideas scattered among his many monographs on a variety of subjects, Herman Bavinck too has also made important contributions toward the development of a Christian view of culture in his more extensive works too.[32]

Moreover, additional work in this field of the Christianization of culture has further been done by the Dutchmen Schilder[33] and Ridderbos[34] and Douma;[35] by the South Africans Stoker[36] and Ven-

---

26. Grosheide, *Culture*, p. 528.
27. Kuyper, *Lectures on Calvinism* (Grand Rapids: Associated Publishers and Authors, Inc., n.d.).
28. Kuyper, *De Gemeene Gratie*, I-III. For particulars of this book and of all the books mentioned here in notes 29-42, cf. our Bibliography below.
29. Kuyper, *Pro Rege*, I-III.
30. Kuyper, *Ons Program* (Amsterdam: J. H. Kruyt, 1879).
31. Kuyper, *Antirevolutionaire Staatkunde* (Kampen: J. H. Kok, 1916), I-II.
32. Cf. Bavinck, *Algemene Genade; Calvin and Common Grace; De Wijsbegeerte der Openbaring; Levensvragen; Bilderdijk als Dichter*; etc.
33. Cf. Schilder, *Wat is de Hemel?; De Openbaring van Johannes en Het Sociale Leven; Jezus Christus en het Cultuureleven*; and *Christus en Cultuur*.
34. Cf. Ridderbos, *De Theologische Cultuurbeschouwing van Abraham Kuyper*; and *Rondom het Gemene Gratie Probleem—over gemene-gratie-beschouwingen van Schilder en De Graaf, . . . over Van Til en Barth.*
35. Douma, *Algemene Genade.*
36. Stoker, *Arbeid—Wysgerig Benader; Die Wysbegeerte van die Skeppingsidee; Kultuur en Roeping; Mens en Tegniek Vandag; Iets oor Kultuur en ons Kultuurstryd*; and, together with Potgieter, eds., *Koers in die Krisis*, I-III.

112

ter[37] and Botha;[38] and by the Americans Henry Van Til[39] and Rushdoony[40] and Schaeffer;[41] as well as by certain other scholars too.[42] But a really definitive *program of action* for the Christianization of the whole of culture (to our knowledge) still remains to be written.

It cannot be our intention in a chapter of this brevity to attempt anything like a detailed program for Christian cultural action or (which latter, however, we have already attempted elsewhere).[43] even a Christian Manifesto toward the Christianization of the world In our remaining sentences, however, we shall merely indicate a few basic aims which we should always keep before our eyes in this regard.

First, we are to attempt nothing less than the reduction of every facet of the culture of the whole world to the recognition of the all-embracing Lordship of Jesus Christ. This is the implication of both the dominion charter (Gen. 1:26-28) and the great commission (Matt. 28:19), as Calvin himself so clearly taught.[44]

Second, this will involve not only the vitally important evangelization of the whole world (Mark 16:15) and our own *personal* engagement therein, but, concurrently herewith, it will also involve[45]

---

37. Venter, *'n Calvinistiese Kultuurbeskouing, 1969-1970; Volkslewe en Kultuur; 'n Calvinistiese Kultuurbeskouing, 1965;* and *Kultuur en Versorgingswetenskap.*
38. Botha, *Die Kulturele Revolusie en Suid-Afrika: 'n Analise; Partikuliere Volksorg in die Afrikaanse Volkskultuur;* and *Sosio-kulturele Metavrae.*
39. Henry Van Til, *The Calvinist Concept of Culture.*
40. Rushdoony, *The Biblical Philosophy of History; By What Standard?; The Institutes of Biblical Law.*
41. Schaeffer, *Art and the Bible; The New Super Spirituality.*
42. Cf. the works of Aalders, Bettex, de Bondt, Haitjema, Hepp, Lee, Le Roux, Meeter, Niebuhr, Popma, Potgieter, Tillich, and Van Der Waal in our Bibliography below.
43. Cf. Lee, "Christians of the World, Unite!—The Christian Manifesto of 1969," in *Christian News-American* (Glendale, Calif., May 1969). Cf. Lee, *Communist Eschatology,* pp. 838-850.
44. Cf. Calvin, *Institutes of the Christian Religion,* IV:3:4; and cf. his *Commentary on 1 Corinthians 15:27* (referring back to Ps. 8).
45. Cf. Lee, *The Westminster Confession and Modern Society* (Edinburgh: The Scottish Reformed Fellowship, 1972).

our working for the recognition of the Ten Commandments as the supreme standard not only in the private lives of Christians but also in the public affairs of all nations, including the United States, the Soviet Union, and Red China (that is, in the individual, marital, family, educational, political, social, economic, ecclesiastical, and every other area of our lives). According to the Westminster Larger Catechism, this will include: yielding all obedience and submission to God with the whole man, being careful in all things to please Him (Q. 104); the promotion of the true worship of God and, according to each one's place and calling, the removal of all idolatry (Q. 109); the sanctification of the whole of the sabbath day (Q. 116); submission to all duly constituted authority (Q. 127) and the godly exercise of such authority over others (Q. 129)—so that we may inherit the national-cultural and the agri-cultural land which the Lord our God giveth us! (Ex. 20:12); the preservation of life and the sober use of food, drink, medicines, sleep, labor, and recreation (Q. 135); modesty in apparel, and behavior and diligent labor in our callings (Q. 138); justice in contracts, moderation in the use of worldly goods, and frugality (Q. 141); speaking the truth and freely acknowledging the gifts of others (Q. 144); and a full contentment with our own condition, and a charitable frame of the whole soul towards our neighbor (Q. 147).

Third, we are to discover our own special gifts of God and then— in accordance with our gifts—to become respectively not just specialists who are Christians, but also specialists who develop our specialties in a specifically *Christian* way. Hence as far as possible we need respectively: Christian preachers and Christian preaching, Christian ethicists and Christian ethics, Christian lawyers and Christian laws, Christian economists and Christian economics, Christian artists and Christian art, Christian sociologists and Christian sociology, Christian linguists and Christian language(s), Christian historians and Christian history, Christian philosophers and Christian philosophy, Christian psychologists and Christian psychology, Christian biologists and Christian biology, Christian physicists and Christian physics, Christian engineers and Christian engineering, Christian mathematicians and Christian mathematics, etc., *all* and *only* to the

114

glory of God. We should form Christian professional associations (local, national, and international), as well as infiltrate into and seek to capture control of non-Christian professional associations for Christ's sake in attempting to turn every sphere of human endeavor toward Christ through the power of His indwelling Spirit.

Fourth, the vital cultural resources of the world we must seek to dedicate exclusively to the cause of the Lord Jesus Christ include religion, food, clothing, housing, industry, and money. And the chief areas of the world we must seek to influence immediately are the United States, Europe, the Soviet Union, Red China, and Japan.

Fifth, positive steps to be taken toward extending Christian cultural influence as the Lord enables, are: total Christian involvement (in our churches, in our jobs, with our gifts, and with our opportunities); total Christian witnessing (in every field, in church, by tracts, in politics, etc.); the total Christianization of the whole of life (including recognition of the sphere-sovereignty of church, state, family, business, society, etc.). To help attain this, we must endeavor to promote: the extension of Christian control over all the existing (and creation of new) mass communications media such as television, newspapers, the movies, and radio; support for the free enterprise trading system; the encouragement of both individual and covenantal incentive and accountability to Almighty God; the strengthening of the rights of inheritance; decentralization of government, industry, education, and church life; the Christianization and strengthening of the armed forces; the reduction of the power of humanistic education, political parties, and labor unions; and the massive promotion of *Christian* schools, *Christian* colleges, *Christian* universities, *Christian* political activities, and *Christian* economic bargaining, etc.

Sixth, opposed as we must of necessity be to *all* departures from God's most holy will, it must be recognized that the various non-Christian movements are not all equally bad, and that there are areas in which, by God's common grace, we may cooperate even with some non-Christians in seeking to realize our Christian objectives.

Hence, there should be glad cooperation with Jews and Muslims against all shades of atheism. Without ever compromising our own distinctively Christian views in any areas, if in following the commandments of our God (for example, in moving against communism and/or pornography) we are offered the support of concerned Jews and/or Muslims, etc., we should willingly welcome and utilize such support.

Seventh, however, in all of this, all men should know exactly where we stand. We stand for the *antithesis* between covenant-keeping Christian culture and covenant-breaking worldly culture, whereby, in the words of the Heidelberg Catechism (Q. 32), we "with a free and good conscience fight against sin and the devil in this life, and hereafter reign with Him everlastingly over all creatures." We stand as Christians on the infallible Word of God, which teaches that God the Father has chosen those who become Christians in Christ before the foundation of the world, so that they should become holy and without blame before Him in love; that He has predestinated them unto the adoption of children by Jesus Christ to Himself, according to the good pleasure of His will; that He has made known to them the mystery of His will, according to His good pleasure which He hath purposed in Himself, so "that in the dispensation of the fullness of the times He might gather together in one *all things* in Christ, both which are in heaven, *and which are on earth,* even in Him; and that the God and Father of the Lord Jesus Christ may give them the Spirit of wisdom and revelation in the knowledge of Him, [so] that the eyes of their understanding may be enlightened [so] that they may know what *is* the hope of His *calling,* and what [is] the *riches* of His inheritance in the saints, and what is the *exceeding greatness of His power to us-ward who believe,* according to the working of His *mighty* power which He wrought in Christ when He *raised Him from the dead and set Him at His own right hand in the heavenly places, far above all principality, and power, and might, and dominion,* and every name that is named, not only *in this world,* but also in that which is to come, and *hath put all things under His feet,* and *gave Him to be the Head over all things to the Church,* which is His body, the fullness of *Him that filleth all in all!"* (Eph. 1:3-11, 17-23).

Onward, then, Christian soldiers! Onward to cultural victory!

* * * *, *

Let us now summarize this last chapter, on the harvesting of culture.

First, we saw that inasmuch as communists and evolutionists have made a highly successful bid to capture control of the world's cultural formative powers, and inasmuch as their power even continues to increase to the peril of Christianity, that Christians are just going to *have* to launch a cultural counter-offensive on all fronts in order to survive.

Second, thus seeing that we dare not ignore the cultural challenge, in recapitulating we realized that the *Bible* actually *expects* us to launch such a counter-offensive! For according to Scripture: all true culture is God-grounded and God-created, is the unavoidable result of man's obedient religious response to the Lord, stretches down throughout world history, and makes life meaningful as does nothing else. According to Scripture: culture only expanded after the fall at all—even among the Cainites!—because of the enabling content of the prophecy of the coming Seed of the woman, and was further promoted by the Noachic covenant and the Babylonian dispersion and the subsequent world empires which awaited the advent of the promised Seed. According to Scripture: Christ is that promised Seed, and culture blossomed in His life and as a result of His resurrection and ascension and heavenly session and the outpouring of His Spirit into His earthly people down through the Christian centuries as never before. And according to Scripture: true culture bears fruit for both this life and the next, and Christians are required and expected to develop a Christian culture here and now as part of their reasonable religion.

Third, we saw that we are required to develop a Christian culture from this point onward in this twentieth century, and not to attempt to restore the cultural life of a bygone era. There can be no return to Eden, to the flood, to the exodus, to Calvary, to Pentecost, or even to the Reformation, although, of course, we are to extract the permanent Christian cultural principles and contributions from all these events and build for the future on that basis.

117

Fourth, it was seen that even regarding fallen man's culture, we are to "prove all things, [and to] hold fast to that which is good." The premillennialist Buswell, the amillennialist Van der Waal, and the postmillennialist Boettner all agree on that. The Inter-Varsity Press writer Triton insists that Christians should be foremost in the promotion of culture. And Calvin and Calvinists like Hepp and Van Peursen and Grosheide are in agreement with Isaiah that Christians should willingly adopt the true cultural insights which God Himself sometimes gives even to unbelievers.

Fifth, we noted that we Christians are not, like Tertullian and the later pietists, to avoid the world's culture, nor, like Clement and Origen, uncritically to absorb it, but, like Noah and Melchizedek and Jacob and Joseph and Moses and Joshua and Solomon and Augustine and Calvin and the later Calvinists, to cleanse what is bad but still utilizable in the culture of our age. For the Biblical prophecies themselves testify that the Christian Church is expansively to be enriched by the cultural treasures of all nations, as she more and more inherits the Gentiles and all their riches.

Sixth, it was seen that we will sometimes have to reject the use of some of this world's culture. God's Word tells use to "abstain from all appearance of evil," and the Ten Commandments (in our judgment adequately explained in the Westminster Larger Catechism) suggest what should be avoided. And in addition, we should also avoid utilizing even legitimate cultural phenomena in circumstances which may probably cause our weaker brother to stumble. At the same time, we must stand fast in the liberty with which Christ has made us free, and not unduly accommodate ourselves to the desires of unbelievers.

And lastly, we saw that we ourselves—under God—must work for cultural victory, as did Kuyper and Bavinck and Schilder, and as Stoker and Venter and others are still doing in our own day. We must evangelize the world, subdue the world in terms of the dominion charter, and work for the universal recognition of the Ten Commandments both in private and in public life. We must encourage suitably gifted Christians to enter into all the professions and, by the power of the Holy Spirit, do everything to the glory of God. Without abandoning any area of life or any country from our program, we should concentrate particularly on religion, food, clothing, housing, industry, and money especially in the United States, Europe, the Soviet Union, Red China, and Japan. We must seek to Christianize particularly the mass communications media, support free enterprise, and to work for the establishment or extension of Christian educational institutions and political activity, while cooperating with all friendly non-Christians who would help us in all this. For on the basis of the incarnation, death, resurrection, ascension, and heavenly session of our Lord Jesus, all things in heaven and on earth are even now being gathered together by His Spirit-filled earthly body—the people of God!

* * * * *

What should we learn from all this here and now, as we again resolve to harvest the world's culture for Jesus' sake?

First, seeing how successful evolutionists and communists have been in capturing control of so many of the cultural formative powers of the world, we should seriously attempt to do the same, for Christ's sake. As Jesus taught: "The children of this world [or the unbelievers] are in their generation [or: in the spheres in which they move] wiser than the children of the light [or the Christians]. And I say unto you, 'Make to yourselves friends of the mammon of unrighteousness; [so] that, when ye fail [or fade away and die], they [the inhabitants of heaven] may receive you into everlasting habitations! He that is faithful in that which is least, is faithful also in much: and he that is unjust in the least, is unjust also in much. If therefore ye have not been faithful in the unrighteous mammon, who will commit to your trust the true riches? And if ye have not been faithful in that which is another man's [namely, Christ's, Who gives us stewardship over *His* goods while we are here on earth], who shall give you that which is your *own* [namely, our own everlasting cultural reward in glory for having multiplied our God-given talents while here on earth]?' " (Luke 16:8-12; cf. II Tim. 4:7-8).

Second, we should not only be as zealous in developing our own Christian culture as the unbelievers are in developing their non-Christian culture, but we should also judiciously borrow whatever we need from non-Christian culture, while purifying it and then gratefully incorporating it into our own Christian cultural system. For as the Second Helvetic Confession tells us: "God in His mercy has permitted the powers of the intellect to remain, though differing greatly from what was in man before the fall. God commands us to cultivate our natural talents, and meanwhile adds both gifts and success. And it is obvious that we make no progress in all the arts without God's blessing. In any case, Scripture refers all the arts to God; and, indeed, the heathen trace the origin of the arts to the gods who invented them."[46]

And lastly, as Christ's blood-bought children, we should regard our pursuit and enjoyment of culture for Jesus' sake as an indispensable means to the chief and highest end of man. For, in the famous words of the Westminster Larger Catechism: "Man's chief and highest end is to glorify God, and *fully* to enjoy Him for ever!"[47]

* * * * *

"Lord, Thou has been our dwelling place *in all generations*. . . . So teach us to number our days, that we may apply our hearts unto *wisdom!* . . . O satisfy us early with Thy mercy; that we may *rejoice* and be *glad* all our days. . . . Let Thy *work* appear unto Thy servants, and Thy glory *unto their children*. And let the *beauty* of the Lord our God be upon us: and *establish* Thou the *work of our hands* upon us; yea, *the work* of our hands, establish Thou it!" (Ps. 90:1, 12, 14, 16-17).

---

46. *Second Helvetic Confession*, chap. IX.
47. *Westminster Larger Catechism*, Q. 1.

Appendix I

Religion and Culture

(From F. N. Lee's "Godsdiens en Kultuur" [Cape Town, South Africa: National Publishers], in *Die Kerkbode,* Feb. 14, 1971, pp. 264-266 [author's own translation])

It is of the uttermost importance *properly to distinguish* terms such as: religion, the service of God (*Godsdiens*), idolatry (*afgodsdiens*), culture, differentiation, decadence, civilization, stimulation, renewal, and Christian culture.

Religion is the binding tendency in every man to dedicate himself with his whole heart either to the true God or to an idol. In this sense all men are religious, for every man dedicates his powers to some or other object of worship, either consciously or unconsciously. The Christian dedicates himself to *Christ,* the Jew to *Judaism,* the Muslim to *Allah,* the communist to *dialectical materialism,* the miser to his *money,* the art-worshiper to his *art,* the lecher to *sex,* the chauvinist to *pseudo-patriotism,* etc. Over a short period of time a particular person may even dedicate himself to more than one object of worship. Thus a Christian may unfortunately dedicate himself to Christ *and* to his business endeavors outside of Christ (as opposed to his business endeavors subject to the will of Christ), and the communist may dedicate himself to communism *and* to his country outside of communism (as opposed to his country subject to communism). But in the long run, when these interests clash, he will *have to choose* between them. Some people are also more intensely religious than others, but all people are religious to some extent and have some or other religion. And so every man at the deepest level is dedicating himself either to God or to an idol. For as the words of Christ remind us: "No man can serve *two* masters: for *either* he will hate the one, and love the other; *or else* he will hold to the one and despise the other" (Matt. 6:24a).

121

True religion (*Godsdiens* = serving the true God) is man's (religious) dedication of the whole of his being, in all that he does, specifically to the *one true God*. Only the Christian religion constitutes the service of the one true God, and only the Christian is truly religious (*Godsdienstig*). Strictly speaking, the religious or dedicated non-Christian should never be described as (truly) religious or as dedicated to the one true God, but only as "idolatrous" (or dedicated to an idol). And inasmuch as God should be served at all times and in all things, it is clear that to be truly religious we must *serve* the one true God not just in the ecclesiastical sphere, but also in the political, scientific, economic, social, and all other spheres (cf. James 1:26-27). The widespread restriction of "serving the Lord" (*Godsdiens*) only to church services, is indeed blasphemous, and only promotes the "dereligification" or secularization of that (major) part of human life which falls outside of church services. Christ commanded: "Thou shalt love the Lord thy God with *all* thy heart, and with *all* thy soul, and with *all* thy mind" (Matt. 22:37) [which surely implies: with *all*-of thy time!]. Only he who regards his serving of the Triune God as the *summum bonum* or as the "highest aim" of his whole life (cf. Ps. 73:25), is to any extent truly religious.

Idolatry or the service of a false god is man's (religious) dedication of part or the whole of his life to *anything* except the one true Triune God. There are different kinds of idols, such as, for example: Allah, my-country-right-or-wrong, science, my-church, my-wife, my-husband, our-children, prestige, art, my-own-future, political-power, culture, my-attending-the-next-big-football-game, money, sports, security, sex, my-family, etc., but all the various kinds of idolatry nevertheless agree with one another in that the service of a *creature* rather than of the *Creator* is made our highest aim in life (Phil. 3:19; Col. 3:5). We should, of course, love all of God's creatures, as well as love their Creator. But we should only love God's creatures *because* they are *God's* creatures and for *His* sake, and never love them in themselves and independently of our loving Him—for *that* is *idolatry!* Idolaters are they who have "changed the truth of God into a lie, and worshipped and served the creature more than the Creator, Who is blessed for ever" (Rom. 1:25). The Gospel must be preached to them, that they "should turn from these vanities unto the living God, Which made heaven, and earth, and the sea, and all things that are therein" (Acts 14:15). For in the long run, all idolatry is vain and (self-) destructive. "Their idols are silver and gold, the work of men's hands. They have mouths, but they speak not: eyes have they, but they see not: they have ears, but they hear not: noses have they, but they smell not: they have hands, but they handle not: feet have they, but they walk not: neither speak they through their throat. They that make them are like unto them; so is every one that trusteth in them" (Ps. 115).

Culture is the unavoidable result of man's necessary efforts to use and to develop the world in which he lives *either* under the guidance of the Lord *or* under the influence of sin, in accordance with whichever of the two controls his heart. As such, culture includes all of man's works—his art, his science, his agriculture, his literature, his language, his astronomical investigations, his rites of worship, his domestic life, his social customs—in short, the cultural products of the whole of man's life stand *either* in the service of God *or* in the service of an idol or idols. "So God created man in His own image, in the image of God created He him; male and female created He them. And God blessed them and God said unto them, 'Be fruitful, and multiply, and replenish the earth, and subdue it: and have dominion over the fish of the sea, and over the fowl of the air, and over every living thing that moveth upon the earth' " (Gen. 1:27-28).

Differentiation (in the sense of the formation of various cultures) is the result of the development of human culture after the fall under the pluriform direct and indirect guidance of God. Even in spite of the fall, human culture would have unfolded differentiatedly in obedience to the dominion charter (Gen. 1:28; 2:24). But after the fall, the dynamic unfolding of this differentiation temporarily lagged until God dynamically effected the development of the differentiated variety of nations and cultures at the tower of Babel as a result of a special act of His common grace (Gen. 11). "When the Most High divided to the nations their inheritance, when He separated the sons of Adam, He set the bounds of the people" (Deut. 32:8). "And [He] hath made of one blood all nations of men for to dwell on all the face of the earth, and hath determined the times before appointed, and the bounds of their habitation; that they should seek the Lord. . . . For in Him we live, and move, and have our being" (Acts 17:26-28).

Decadence or cultural retrogression is the result of the fall and of the further operation of its consequences. Wherever fallen man succumbs to the influence of a radically sinful religious basic motive, and wherever God to some extent withdraws His common grace from man and his culture, he (and ultimately even his culture) becomes decadent. Decadence not only occurs among so-called primitive cultures (as, for example, those in the Congo), but it also occurs among very developed cultures too (as, for example, among the hippies in the West). And just as there was a decadent period of culture right before the flood, so too shall there also be a more sophisticated and worldwide cultural decadence later toward the end of history (Luke 17:26-30; Rev. 20:7-9; cf. too Gen. 6:1-8 and II Pet. 3:3-13).

Civilization or cultural maturity is the result of the operation of God's common grace (and sometimes even of His saving or special grace too) in human society in spite of the fall. Not all (un)believers and their cultures are (un)developed. Even among the (un)believers and their societies, the Spirit distributes His (cultural) gifts as He wishes (cf. I Cor. 12:4-11; Job 32:8; Eph. 4:8; I Pet. 4:10). As a matter of fact, the first culture after the fall which developed into a civilization was that of Cain and his ungodly descendants and *not* that of the believing descendants of Seth. But even among the Cainites, culture only developed as a result of the (non-saving) gracious operation of the Spirit of God Who arrested the further expansive penetration of sin and Who distributed all those cultural gifts and Who caused them to unfold. "But there is a spirit in man: and the inspiration of the Almighty giveth them understanding" (Job 32:8). "The spirit of man is the candle of the Lord, searching all the inward parts of the belly" (Prov. 20:27; cf. Rom. 2:15). "And Adah bare Jabal: he was the father of such as dwell in tents, and of such as have cattle. And his brother's name was Jubal: he was the father of all such as handle the harp and organ. And Zillah, she also bare Tubal-cain, an instructor of every artificer in brass and iron. . . . And the Lord said, 'My Spirit shall not always strive with man [or: rule in man]' " (Gen. 4:20-22; 6:3).

Stimulation of cultures results as a consequence of contact with other cultures with a higher standard of civilization. In this way the declining slave culture of the Israelites was stimulated prior to the exodus as a result of contact with the Egyptian civilization, when the Israelites "borrowed [the] treasures of Egypt" (Heb. 11:26 cf. Acts 7:22 and Ex. 11:2; 12:35-36). Such stimulation can, however, be very dangerous—as, for example, is evident from the episode of the golden calf (Ex. 32:1-4) and also from the early Middle Ages when the developing Christian culture was injuriously stimulated by the mighty Greek civilization and thus degenerated into the Romish civilization (cf. Col. 2:8-23!). As the Lord Jesus Himself remarked: "Ye cannot serve God *and* mammon!" (Matt. 6:24b).

Renewal of mature cultures happens as a result of a religious revival or conscious rediscovery of the religious roots of the culture concerned. Thus, for example, was the declining culture of the Israelites renewed in the wilderness, when the Holy Spirit laid hold on the cultural gifts and on the hearts of Bezaleel and Aholiab (Ex. 31:1-6 and 35:5, 21-25).

Christian culture develops where the formers of culture consciously acknowledge the Word and the Spirit of God as the motive forces behind a particular cultural development. Then every branch of human culture is governed by the triune Christian basic religious motive of creation-fall-consummation (Col. 1:9-22 cf. Rom.11:33-36).

What we therefore need today is: (1) the rejection of all false systems of culture; (2) the adoption and adaptation of all the true elements to be found therein; (3) the repudiation of all attempts to synthesize Christian culture and non-Christian culture; and (4) the powerful development of consistently Christian culture in every field of endeavor.

To this end, every Christian must *totally* disengage himself from humanism and learn how to eat and to drink and to do *all* things "to the glory of God" (cf. I Cor. 10:31).

Is *this* also *your* aim?

Appendix II

May Man Dominate the Moon?

(From F. N. Lee's "Maanreise en die Kultuurmandaat," published as "Die Maan—Verbode Terrein vir die Mens?" in *Die Kerkbode*, Cape Town, South Africa, Oct. 15, 1969)

Unavoidably the moon landings have ignited discussion among Christians as to the propriety of these endeavors. Many believers are now asking questions such as: *Should* man go to the moon? (cf. Rom. 14:23). *Is* that glorifying to God? (cf. I Cor. 10:31). What saith the *Scripture?* (cf. Rom. 4:3).

Scripture teaches that only God the Creator is eternal (Ps. 90:1-2; Prov. 8:22-31), and that both the heavens and the earth are only different areas of one and the same time-bound creation. As such they represent *one created whole* (Gen. 1:1; Col. 1:16; Rev. 4:11; 10:6; 14:7; 22:2). And this time-bound and unitary creation, in spite of all the differences between the heavens and the earth, is upheld by one continuous divine deed in creating (Ps. 33:6-9; Jer. 10:10-16) and unfolding (Gen. 1:3-2:3; Ex. 20:11) and maintaining (Gen. 1:14-18; Jer. 31:35-37) and redeeming (Eph. 1:10, 20-22; Col. 1:20) and consummating (Isa. 66; Rev. 22) the entire universe as a whole.

Scripture also teaches that the Lord *created man in the image of God* (Gen. 1:26-27; 9:6; James 3:9). Because man is only the *image* of God and not God Himself, man's dominion is not sovereign but dependent upon God. There are indeed places where man does not yet—and perhaps never will—wield even a dependent dominion (Eccles. 5:2; Job 38–42, and esp. 38:26). Yet as the image of the King eternal or Monarch of the ages (*Basileus tōn aiōnōn*) and as the likeness of the Ruler of the world-process, man has the ages of the world (*'olām*) in his heart (I Tim. 1:17; Eccles. 3:11). Consequently, as the image of the Creator of the earth and the heavens (*hashshamāyim*—Gen. 1:1), man was created out of earthly matter yet with a "heavenly" created spirit (Gen. 2:7; Eccles. 3:21; 12:7; Zech. 12:1; I Cor. 15:40-49; II Cor. 4:16-5:9; Rev. 4:1 cf. 6:9 and 20:1, 4). And as the image of the Dominator of the earth and the heavens, (faithful) man too is destined to dominate the earth and the heavens under God and as His agent (Gen. 1:26-28; Rev. 12:1). This man is to do in terms of the so-called *dominion charter* —for this divine command not only requires man to subdue the earth, but it also stipulates that he is to dominate the fishes of the sea and the birds of the air or the *heavens* (*hashshamāyim*—Gen. 1:26).

On account of the *fall,* however, man as the image of God in the narrower sense of the word has now become totally depraved; but in spite of this, even fallen man still remains the image of God in the broader sense of the word, and consequently he is still required to obey the dominion charter (Gen. 1:28; 5:1-3; 9:1-6; Ps. 8; James 3:7-9; Heb. 2:6-8). By virtue of God's *common grace,* it is still possible for even *un*regenerate fallen man (and by God's *particular grace* even more possible for *re*generate man)—at least to some extent (Job 38:25-35; 9:1-9; chs. 26–28)—progressively more and more to subdue the earth and the sea and even the heavens: as man's successful journeys to the moon so clearly prove! But even all this is possible only on account of the cosmos-embracing scope of the *protevangelium* or first gospel promise which bridled man's total depravity immediately after the fall (Gen. 2:15-17; 3:11-20).

By virtue of this *first gospel promise,* the Son of God became the Second Adam in the fullness of time (Gal. 4:4-5; I Cor. 15:22-26, 45-47). He executed the dominion charter by subduing the earth and the sea *and the heavens* as the Son of *man* (Mark 1:13; Matt. 8:23f.; 27:45; 28:18; Heb. 2:6-10; I Cor. 15:22-28). And it is *His* ascension into heaven far beyond the moon (and without the aid of any space ship!)—not to speak of His future second coming on the clouds of heaven with power and great glory!—which enables us to see the very much lesser American and Russian space achievements in their true perspective (Eph. 4:8-10; Acts 1:9-11; Rev. 1:7).

127

On the basis of *this cosmos-embracing work of the Second Adam Jesus Christ,* graciously imputed to the Christian (and not without some non-saving benefits even to the reprobate), the believer is already in principle the restored image of God in the narrower sense of the word, and he already in principle sits in the heavenly places (Luke 11:2; 17:20-21; Eph. 2:6). When he dies, the soul of the believer goes to heaven immediately (Rev. 4:1-8; 5:9-10; 6:9-11; 7:9-17)—and it will finally be restored to its earthly body when the believer will rule over the renewed earth as God's viceroy (Matt. 5:5; Rev. 21-22).

For this reason, John Calvin, the greatest of all the Protestant Reformers, already gave some thought to man's present vocation to subdue the heavenly bodies by means of scientific research. While strongly rejecting *astrology* (which would subdue human knowledge to the heavenly bodies) as a "diabolical illusion" (Commentary on Dan. 1:4; cf. Isa. 47:13), he recommended the pursuit of *astronomy* (which would subdue the heavenly bodies to human knowledge). "With painstaking effort the astronomers investigate everything which the wisdom of the human intellect can grasp," wrote Calvin (Commentary on Gen. 1:6); as "it cannot be denied that this art unfolds the admirable wisdom of God." Consequently, astronomers should "be honored as those who have devoted useful labors hereto, so that those who have the time and abilities *should not neglect this* kind of exercise." "To investigate the movements of the heavenly bodies, to determine their positions, to measure their distances and to determine their properties, demands scholarly and careful study. And whereas these things are so arranged that the Providence of God is more fully unfolded thereby, it is reasonable to presuppose that the understanding undertakes a loftier flight and obtains clearer views of His Glory" (*Institutes* I:5:2). "To give evidence of His wonderful wisdom, both the heavens and the earth give us untold proofs—proofs which astronomy, medicine and all the natural sciences are developed to illustrate." What is more, these "arts and sciences we received from the heathen. We are indeed forced to acknowledge that it is from them that we received . . . astronomy. And neither may it be doubted that God so enriched them with liberal favors, so that their godlessness might be so much the less excusable" (Commentary on Gen. 4:20).

It is clear, then, that the dominion charter (whereby man is to subdue, among other things, even the birds of *the heavens*), which was given to man at his creation and which was also frequently repeated to him even *after* the fall, embraces the subduing not only of the earth but *of the heavens too!* And therefore Calvin was also correct when, more than four centuries ago (!), he remarked about the dominion charter (as repeated in the eighth psalm of David) that "the Prophet (David) does indeed mention 'birds of the heaven,' 'fish of the sea,' and 'beasts of the field,' because this kind of dominion [of man thereover] is visible and more conspicuous; but at the same time the general statement stretches *much* further—even to *the heavens* and the earth and *everything they contain*" (Commentary on I Cor. 15:27, referring back to Ps. 8). God gave cosmic dominion over *all* created things to men once and for all, because, maintains Calvin, "He predestinated *all the riches* both of *the heavens* and the earth *for their use*" (Commentary on Ps. 8:6).

So, then—as far as humanly possible (and whatever is humanly possible is so only by divine pre-ordination!), let us: harness the solar energy of the sun; incinerate our trash on Mercury; colonize Venus; mine the moon; vacation on Mars; exploit the natural gas on Jupiter; pipe the oil (if any) from Saturn; extract the gold from Uranus; transfer our cold storage to Neptune; and build our refueling stations on Pluto as we launch out ever farther into this gigantic universe which God has created for the use of man!

Throughout the Scriptures, the possibility even of *human space travel* is presupposed. Think, for example, of Enoch, and especially of Elijah (Gen. 5:22-24; Heb. 11:5; Jude 14-15; II Kings 2:1, 11; cf. Kuyper: *Dict. Dogm.*, 2nd ed., II, loc de hom., para. 13, and *Van de Voleinding*, I, p. 256, n. 1, 1929 ed., who connects Gen. 1:28 with 5:22-24, etc.). It is perfectly true that in an indirect way Scripture possibly also anticipates the dangers of all celestial undertakings conceived in human pride (cf. Gen. 11:1-9; Job 20:5-9; Obad. 3-4). But this is also true of all *earthly* endeavors conducted with a high heart! (cf. Isa. 3:16-26; Luke 12:13-21). Hence, the farmer ploughing his fields without reference to God (cf. Prov. 21:4), and the apostate preacher who cheapens the precious gospel (II Pet. 2:1 cf. James 3:1), greatly displease Almighty God in so doing—whereas if space travelers consciously glorify God in their exploits (as did Enoch, Elijah, and Jesus!), these deeds cannot possibly have been divinely forbidden.

To the contrary, the permissibility of human journeys into space is rather presupposed in that the Lord has crowned man with glory and honor as the viceroy over the entire creation in terms of the dominion charter (Ps. 8:3-6; Heb. 2:7-8; cf. Ps. 139:8, 14). The coronation of man glorified the entire creation. The fall of this crowned being besmirched the whole universe over which he was and is to reign. And the restoration of crowned man—in principle already accomplished through the finished work of Christ as the Second Adam—re-glorified and is progressively more and more still re-glorifying the entire creation (Rom. 8:19-29 cf. Ps. 8). If, then, as Calvin stated, "the *condemnation* of humanity has been *impressed upon the heavens*" (Commentary on Rom. 8:19), it is only to be expected (on the basis of God's common and/or particular grace) that *man's achievements too* are capable of being impressed upon the heavens!

May man then go to the moon? *No!*—if by so doing he wishes to defy the Lord; for *everything* man undertakes should be done only to the glory of God. But *yes!*—according to the still valid cosmos-embracing dominion charter that has so frequently been repeated even after the fall; *provided* man desires to glorify God in so doing. And man may also travel *much farther* than just to the moon! As David prayed to the Lord: "When I consider *Thy heavens*, the work of Thy fingers, *the moon* and *the stars*, which Thou hast ordained: What is man, that Thou art mindful of him? . . . Thou hast made him a little lower than a *divine being* (*mē'elôhīm*), and *hast crowned him* with glory and honour. Thou madest him to *have dominion* over the works of Thy hands; Thou hast put *all things* [thus including even the afore-mentioned sun and moon and stars!] under his feet" (Ps. 8:3-6). Moreover, in the last book of the Bible, the apostle John tells us that the Christian Church is not only *crowned with stars,* but also that she *dominates the moon* under her feet (Rev. 12:1). And however symbolically these words should doubtlessly be interpreted, one can hardly eliminate the clear implications which they *also* bear in terms of man's cosmos-embracing dominion charter which they presuppose as their ultimate foundation.

Too long have Russian communists and the more humanistic element of American society virtually monopolized space. May Bible-believing Christians, particularly here in the nominally Christian West, ignited by the Holy Spirit, take the dominion charter much more seriously even in respect of the conquest of space—all and only to the glory of God!

Appendix III

Will Our Present Works Be Preserved on the New Earth?

Had man never fallen into sin, Adam would still have preached to his children and exhorted them to obey, but not, of course, to repent (thus Luther, as quoted in Lee, *The Covenantal Sabbath*, pp. 77-78; cf. Gen. 1:26-28; 2:1-3); and in glory, preachers (and others too) will undoubtedly proclaim the mighty deeds of God (cf. Rev. 4:8f.–5:14), and do many other things as well. Had man never fallen into sin, at least some of Adam's children would have built ships and become sailors and interlinked the continents after men would have gone forth from Eden populating the ends of the earth (Gen. 1:28; 2:24); and in glory, even if (!) there will be literally "no more sea" (Rev. 22:1), there will still be commercial traffic (Rev. 21:24-26 cf. 7:15-17)—which is what sailors are now engaged in—and possibly even river shipping! (Rev. 22:1f. cf Isa. 60:6-9).

We are certainly not saying, then, that life on the new earth will be exactly the way it is now, merely minus sin. Indeed, none of us during this present life can form an altogether accurate picture of the nature of our life in the world to come. Nor are we saying that life on the new earth will be exactly the way it was in Eden before the fall. Nor are we even saying that life on the new earth will be exactly the way earthly life would ultimately have become under Adam's stewardship, had sin never occurred. But we are most definitely saying that God preordained and therefore respects history; and that many of the elements and products of culture now being developed shall (albeit in a new and a cleansed form) be preserved for all eternity on the new earth to come.

Of course, professions which are sinful in themselves, such as prostitution and gambling operations and pornography production

132

and robbery—which would never have been engaged in, had man not fallen—will hardly yield anything of eternal value for the life on the new earth to come.

However, it is easy to see how the present earthly work of the Christian preacher and the Christian theologian and the Christian musician and the Christian philosopher has permanent value for all eternity. For all the professions engaged in by these men would have developed even if the fall had never taken place (although they would then, of course, have developed somewhat differently). And even though it is not always easy for us to see the permanently valuable features in the present earthly work of the Christian garbage collector and the Christian policeman and the Christian surgeon and the Christian soldier—all professions which would hardly have developed had Satan and men never fallen into sin—no one will dispute the great value of the work produced by these professions in this present world. And even if the present *products* of these professions (such as trash dumps and jails and appendectomies and violence) will not be utilized on the new earth to come, the present *knowledge* thus being acquired, will even then be preserved. For knowledge of cleanliness and hygiene or of law and order or of health and physiology or of discipline and victory will even then be preserved. And irrespective of their present vocations, all of God's children will then develop in other directions too unto all eternity—by utilizing the permanent accumulation of all of man's culture now being produced, and also by developing culture even further during the life to come.

Clearly, then, however modified in its operation, the dominion charter *continues* even in glory (Gen. 1:28 cf. Rev. 22:3, 5). Doubtless there is merit in distinguishing *culture* as the human *work* performed from cultural *products* as the result of that work (thus C. N. Venter, *'n Calvinistiese Kultuurbeskouing*, in *Die Atoomeeu in U Lig*, pp. 313-315), so that our thus-defined "culture" here and now would still yield eschatologically permanent fruit, even if and even where our present cultural "products" may be transitory. Yet Kuyper has correctly insisted (in his *Gemeene Gratie*, I, pp. 358-498), "holding fast to the lines of Revelation 14:13, that if we die in Christ our toils and our labors terminate at death; but that our *works,* that is, the fruits or acquisitions or results of our labor, accompany us unto everlasting life. . . .—not only our *spiritual* but also our ordinary human acquisitions . . ." (*ibid.,* p. 472).

Also, the "honor and glory" of the nations (according to Rev. 21:24-26) to be brought into the New Jerusalem, says Kuyper, will come from "the English and the German" nations and "from Venezuela or Argentina" and even from the ancient "Egyptians and Babylonians" and "the Greeks and the Romans"—implying "that these acquisitions (*winste*) do not simply pass away and become annihilated in the general conflagration of the world, but that they will have a permanent significance even for the New Jerusalem, i.e., for the new earth" (pp. 464-465).

Moreover, adds Kuyper (*Van de Voleinding,* IV, pp. 390-392), the fact that the tree of life will grow on the new earth, and that "the leaves of the tree are for the healing of the nations" (Rev. 22:2b), insures that the cultural disparity between one individual and another and between one nation and others here and now on earth will then be smoothed away on the new earth to come. But even thereafter, our human life on the new earth will never freeze into monotony and uniformity, century after century. For there will always be an ever-richer culture to which saved humanity will be able to aspire even on the new earth (Rev. 22:4).

On this latter point, Okke Jager well says (in his *Het Eeuwige Leven,* esp. pp. 561-578): "Wielenga speaks of 'development and achievement, becoming and being, garden and city' in Rev. 22:2" (p. 561). "If our everlastingness were not to be conscious of a succession of moments, we would not be able to speak here of the possibility of seeing the wounds in Jesus' hands at a definite moment and of thereafter again drinking the new wine. The word 'Lamb' in the final chapters of the Bible already points to the continuity of time. The 'Lamb' constantly makes us look backward and look forward. . . . In the end time (on the new earth), man in his genuine humanity will be directed toward God, his fellowman, and the cosmos. And this position will exclude all deification or eternalization [of man]. . . . If man the creature is *not* then to live in time, where *will* he *live? Then* he would have to be absorbed into God. Only by confessing the continuity of time, are we armed against pantheism" (*ibid.*, p. 577).

Moreover, it seems to this present writer (Francis Nigel Lee) that man in his glory will not merely enjoy the cultural fruits of this present life here and now (Matt. 5:5; Rev. 14:13; 21:24-26), but that he will also constantly increase in glory as he continues to produce new cultural products on the new earth forever. For at the *resurrection* of all flesh at the end of history (Dan. 12:1-3; Luke 11:31-32; John 5:24-29), those resurrected unto glory will at first only correspond to the humanity of the *resurrected* Christ. But just as the *resurrected* Christ was even more glorified at His later *ascension* and still more so at His yet later heavenly *session* and is thereafter and even now *still expanding His rule in glory* down through the Christian centuries (Luke 24:26; John 20:17; Eph. 1:19-22; 2:5-7; I Cor. 15:24-28; Rev. 1:6-7)—so too, it seems, will future-glorified man also progressively increase *from* glory *unto* glory respectively at his *resurrection,* his *ascension,* his heavenly *session,* and his *expansion* of his rule-together-with-Christ down through all the never-ending sub-sequent "centuries" too on the new earth to come (I Cor. 15:42-52; II Cor. 3:18; I Thess. 4:15-17; Phil. 3:20-21; I Cor. 6:2-3; Isa. 65–66; Rev. 21:24-26; 22:1-5). For at that time and forever there-after, glorified man will not only partake of the fruit of the tree of life every *month,* but he will also *rule* with the Lord and *serve* Him forever (Rev. 22:2, 3, 4, 5; Ps. 36:7-10; II Cor. 3:18). Clearly, then, there is no question of any *stagnation* in glory; neither should God's children stagnate here and now!

Realizing all this, then—*the daily work now being performed here on earth to the glory of God by every Christian, irrespective of his profession, should become more meaningful to him each day, because somehow or other its permanent value will be preserved and enjoyed on the new earth forever, and perhaps even form the basis of his yet future works which he will commence doing at that future time.*

"But as it is written, 'Eye hath not seen, nor ear heard, neither have entered into the heart of man, the things which God hath prepared for them that love Him.' But God hath revealed them unto us by His Spirit. . . . But we all, with open face beholding as in a [looking] glass the glory of the Lord, are changed into the same image *from* glory *to* glory, even as by the Spirit of the Lord. . . . And they shall see His face . . . and they shall reign for ever and ever!" (I Cor. 2:9-10; II Cor. 3:18; Rev. 22:4-5).

A SELECT BIBLIOGRAPHY
Of Over One Hundred Writings Pertaining to Culture

Aalders, G. Ch. *De Goddelijke Openbaring in de eerste drie hoofd-stukken van Genesis* (The Divine Revelation in the first three chapters of Genesis). Kampen, Netherlands: J. H. Kok, 1932.

————. *Het Verbond Gods* (The Covenant of God). Kampen, Netherlands: J. H. Kok, 1939.

Aalders, W. J. *Cultuur en Sacrament* (Culture and Sacrament).

————. *Reformatie en Cultuur* (Reformation and Culture).

————. *Roeping en Beroep bij Calvijn* (Vocation and Career in Calvin). Groningen, Netherlands, 1943.

————. *Van Godsdienst en Leven* (On Religion and Life). Putten, Netherlands: Terwee, 1929.

Baillie. *What Is a Christian Civilization?* London, England, 1948.

Barth. *Der Christ in der Gesellschaft* (The Christian in Society). Munich, Germany, 1920.

————. *Kirche und Kultur* (Church and Culture). Amsterdam, Netherlands, 1926.

Bavinck. *Algemene Genade* (Common Grace). Kampen, Netherlands, 1894.

————. *Bilderdijk als Denker en Dichter* (Bilderdijk as a Thinker and as a Poet). Kampen, Netherlands: J. H. Kok, 1906.

————. "Calvin and Common Grace," in *The Princeton Theological Review* VII, no. 3 (1909).

————. *De Catholiciteit van Christendom en Kerk* (The Catholicity of Christianity and the Church). Kampen, Netherlands: J. H. Kok, 1888.

————. *Levensvragen* (Vital Issues). Kampen, Netherlands: J. H. Kok, 1929.

————. "Revelation and Culture," in his *Stone Lectures.*

————. *Wijsbegeerte der Openbaring* (The Philosophy of Revelation). Kampen, Netherlands: J. H. Kok, 1907.

Berkhof. *Christ the Meaning of History.* Richmond, Va.: John Knox Press, 1966.

————. *De Mens Onderweg—een Christelijke mensbeschouwing* (Man Under Way—A Christian View of Man). 's-Gravenhage, Netherlands: Boekencentrum N.V., 1965.

Berkouwer. *De mens het beeld Gods* (Man the Image of God). Kampen, Netherlands: J. H. Kok, 1957.

Bettex. *Beschaving* (Civilization). Amsterdam, Netherlands. and Pretoria, South Africa: Höveker & Wormser, n.d.

Biesterveld. *Christendom en Cultuur* (Christianity and Culture). Kampen, Netherlands: J. H. Kok, 1900.

Black. *Culture and Restraint.* London, England: Hodder & Stoughton, 1901.

Blocher. "God's Mandate and Man's Response," *International Reformed Bulletin* (Winter/Spring, 1973).

Bohatec. "Die Kultuurhistoriese Betekenis van Calvyn" ("The Cultural Historical Significance of Calvin"), in Stoker and Potgieter, eds., *Koers in die Krisis* (q.v.), II.

Botha. *Die Kulturele Revolusie en Suid-Afrika* (The Cultural Revolution and South Africa). Potchefstroom, South Africa: Institute for the Promotion of Calvinism, n.d., no. 68.

————. *Partikuliere Volksorg in die Afrikaanse Volkskultuur, 1930–1964* (Particular National Welfare in the South African National Culture, 1930–1964). Potchefstroom, South Africa: Potchefstroom University for Christian Higher Education.

————. *Sosio-kulturele Metavrae* (Socio-cultural Meta-questions). Amsterdam, Netherlands: Buijten & Schipperheijn, 1971.

Brunner. *Christianity and Civilization*, vols. I-II. London, England: James Nisbet, 1948. ·

Buddingh. *Cultuur en Communicatie* (Culture and Communication). Aalten, Netherlands: N.V. Uitgeversmaatschappij De Graafschap, n.d.

Caillet. *The Christian Appraisal of Culture.* New York, 1953.

———. *The Christian Approach to Culture.* Nashville, Tenn.: Abingdon Press, 1953.

Calder. *After the Seventh Day: The World Man Created.* New York: Mentor, 1961.

Clowney. "Transmitting Christian Culture," in *Christian Home and School* (November, 1952).

Coetzee. "Die Calvinistiese Bydrae tot die Kunsontwikkeling in die Wêreld" ("The Calvinistic Contribution Toward the Development of Art in the World"), in Stoker and Potgieter, eds., *Koers in die Krisis* (q.v.), II.

Danhof & Hoeksema. *Van Zonde en Genade* (Concerning Sin and Grace). Kalamazoo, Mich.: Dalm Printing Co., n.d.

Dawson. *Religion and Culture.* New York, 1947.

De Bondt. "De Algemene Genade" ("General Grace"), in Berkouwer & Toornvliet, *Het Dogma der Kerk* (The Teaching of the Church). Groningen, Netherlands: Jan Haan, 1949.

———. "Schepping en Voorzienigheid" ("Creation and Providence"), in Berkouwer & Toornvliet (cf. De Bondt, "De Algemene Genade").

De Graaf. *Christus en de wereld* (Christ and the World). Kampen, Netherlands: J. H. Kok, 1939.

———. "De genade Gods en de structuur der gansche schepping" ("The Grace of God and the Structure of the Entire Creation"), in *Philosophia Reformata* (Reformed Philosophy), (q.v.), first issue.

Diemer. *Het Scheppingsverbond met Adam* (The Creation Covenant with Adam). Kampen, Netherlands: J. H. Kok, n.d.

Diepenhorst. *Algemeene Genade en Antithese* (Common Grace and Antithesis). Kampen, Netherlands, 1947.

Dijk. "De Leer der Laatsten Dingen" ("The Doctrine of the Last Things"), in Berkouwer & Toornvliet (cf. De Bondt).

139

Douma. *Algemene Genade—uiteenzetting, vergelijking en beoordeling van de opvattingen van A. Kuyper, K. Schilder en Joh. Calvijn over 'algemene genade'* (General Grace—exposition, comparison and evaluation of the views of A. Kuyper, K. Schilder and John Calvin on 'General Grace'). Goes, Netherlands: Oosterbaan & Le Cointre, 1966.

Duvenage, B. *Beroepsarbeid in die Lig van die Gereformeerde Etiek* (Career Work in the Light of Reformed Ethics). Potchefstroom, South Africa: Potchefstroom University for Christian Higher Education, n.d.

Duvenage, S. C. W. *Die Beplanning van Werk en Tyd vanuit Calvinistiese Visie* (The Planning of Work and Time from the Calvinistic Perspective). Potchefstroom, South Africa: Institute for the Promotion of Calvinism, no. 7.

Foerster. *Christus en het Menschelijke Leven* (Christ and Human Life). Zeist, Netherlands: Ploegsma, 1925.

Eliot. *Notes Toward a Definition of Culture.* New York, 1949.

———. *The Idea of a Christian Society.* New York, 1940.

Flemming. "Die Calvinisme en die Toneel" ("Calvinism and the Theater"), in Stoker and Potgieter. eds, *Koers in die Krisis* (q.v.), III.

Goedhart. *Christendom en Cultuur* (Christianity and Culture). Woerden, Netherlands: Zuijderduijn, 1963.

Goodman. *The Individual and Culture.* Illinois: The Dorsey Press, 1967.

Grabmann. *Die Kulturphilosophie des Heiligen Thomas von Aquino* (The Cultural Philosophy of St. Thomas Aquinas). Germany, 1925.

Greijdanus. "Kerk en Koninkrijk Gods" ("The Church and the Kingdom of God"), in *Referaten—Rudel Congres van Gereformeerden* (Lectures—Rudel Reformed Congress). Kampen, Netherlands, 1948.

———. "De Verovering der Wereld" ("The Conquest of the World"), in *De Reformatie* (The Reformation). Goes, Netherlands, 1947.

Grosheide. "Cultuur" ("Culture") in *Christelijke Encyclopaedie* (The Christian Encyclopaedia). Kampen, Netherlands: J. H. Kok, 1925.

Haan. *Scripturally-Oriented Higher Education.* Sioux Center, Iowa: Dordt College Press, 1967.

Haitjema. "Abraham Kuyper und die Theologie des holländischen Neucalvinismus" ("Abraham Kuyper and the Theology of Dutch Neo-Calvinism"), in *Zwischen den Zeiten* (Between the Times). Munich, Germany, 1931.

————. "De cultuur-waardering van het Nieuw Calvinisme" ("The Culture Appreciation of Neo-Calvinism"), in *Onze Eeuw* (Our Century), Haarlem, Netherlands, IV (1919).

Hanko. *The Christian and the Film Arts.* Grand Rapids, Mich.: Sunday School Mission Publishing Society, n.d.

Hard. "Missions and the Cultural Mandate," in *International Reformed Bulletin* (Winter, 1972).

Hepp. "De algemeene genade" ("General Grace"), in *Dreigende Deformatie* (Threatening Deformation). Kampen, Netherlands, IV (1937).

Herridge. "Culture," in *The Presbyterian Review* IX.

Hoekendijk. "Het Christendom in de wereldgeschiedenis" ("Christianity in World History"), in *Wending* (Turning). 's-Gravenhage, Netherlands, 1965.

Hoeksema. *In the Midst of Death.* Grand Rapids, Mich.: Eerdmans, 1943.

————. *The Christian and Culture.* Grand Rapids, Mich.: Sunday School Mission Publishing Society, 1956.

————. *The Curse-Reward of the Wicked Well-Doer.* Grand Rapids, Mich.: Sunday School Mission Publishing Society, n.d.

————. *The Protestant Reformed Church in America,* 2nd ed. Grand Rapids, Mich.: Sunday School Mission Publishing Society, 1947—especially Part II, on the "Three Points" of the Christian Reformed Church's Synod's Decisions on "Common Grade."

Hoeksema & Danhof. See Danhof & Hoeksema.

Hommes, *et al. Cultuurgeschiedenis van het Christendom* (Cultural History of Christianity), vols. I-V. Amsterdam, Netherlands, and Brussels, Belgium, 1950.

Ingwersen. *Bijbel en Cultuur* (The Bible and Culture). Hoorn, Netherlands: U. M. West-Friesland, 1947.

————. *Bijbel en Natuur* (The Bible and Nature). Hoorn, Netherlands: U. M. West-Friesland, 1946.

Jager. *Het Eeuwige Leven* (Eternal Life). Kampen, Netherlands: J. H. Kok, 1962.

Kamphuis. *Onderweg Aangesproken: Beschouwingen over Kerk, Confessie en Cultuur* (En Route Addresses: Views on Church, Confession and Culture). Groningen, Netherlands: Uitgeverij De Vuurbaak, 1968.

Klooster. "The Synodical Decisions of 1924 on Common Grace," in *Torch and Trumpet* VIII (November, 1958).

Knuvelder. *Christelijke Cultuur en Techniek* (Christian Culture and Technology).

Kroner. *Culture and Faith.* Chicago, 1951.

Kruyswijk. *De Ongerepte Orde—Schets van een Christelijke Cultuurbeschouwing* (The Virgin Soil—Sketch of a Christian View of Culture). Kampen, Netherlands: J. H. Kok, 1957.

Kuiper, H. *Calvin on Common Grace.* Goes, Netherlands, 1928.

Kuyper, A. *De Gemeene Gratie* (Common Grace). Kampen, Netherlands: J. H. Kok, 1927.

————. *Het Werk van den Heiligen Geest* (The Work of the Holy Spirit). Kampen, Netherlands: J. H. Kok, 1927.

————. *Lectures on Calvinism: The Stone Lectures* (Grand Rapids, Mich.: The Associated Publishers and Authors, Inc., n.d.

————. *Pro Rege, of het Koningschap van Christus* (For the King, or the Kingship of Christ), I-III. Kampen, Netherlands: J. H. Kok, 1911.

————. *Tweërlei Vaderland* (Two Countries). Amsterdam, Netherlands, 1887.

————. *Van de Voleinding* (Concerning the Consummation), I-IV. Kampen, Netherlands: J. H. Kok, 1931.

Kuyper, A., Jr. *De Band des Verbonds* (The Bond of the Covenant). Rotterdam, Netherlands: Zwagers, 1928.

————. *De Vastigheid des Verbonds* (The Firmness of the Covenant). Amsterdam, Netherlands: Kirchner), 1908.

————. *Het Beeld Gods* (The Image of God). Amsterdam, Netherlands: De Standaard, 1929.

————. *Openbaring en Rede* (Revelation and Reason). Kampen, Netherlands: J. H. Kok, 1902.

————. *Van der Heiligmaking, van de Heerlijkmaking, en van het Rijk der Heerlijkheid* (On Sanctification, on Glorification, and on the Kingdom of Glory). Amsterdam, Netherlands: Meinema, 1935.

————. *Van het Koninkryk der Hemelen* (On the Kingdom of Heaven). Kampen, Netherlands: J. H. Kok, 1932.

Lee. *Calvin on the Sciences.* London, England: Sovereign Grace Union, 1969.

————. *Culture—a Theological and Philosophical Analysis of the Origin, Spread and Goal of Culture.* Cape May, N. J.: Shelton College Press, 1967.

————. *Communist Eschatology—A Christian Philosophical Analysis of the Post-Capitalistic Views of Marx, Engels and Lenin.* Nutley, N. J.: The Craig Press, 1974.

————. "Kultuur en Godsdiens" ("Culture and Religion"), in *Die Kerkbode* (The Church Messenger). Cape Town, South Africa (Feb. 21, 1971).

————. "Maanreise en die Kultuurmandaat" ("Journeys to the Moon and the Dominion Charter"), published as "Die Maan—Verbode Terrein vir die Mens?" ("Is the Moon Forbidden Territory to Man?"), in *Die Kerkbode* (The Church Messenger), (Oct. 15, 1969).

————. *The Covenantal Sabbath.* London, England: Lord's Day Observance Society, [n.d.] 1971.

————. *The Origin and Destiny of Man.* Nutley, N. J.: Presbyterian and Reformed Publishing Co., 1974.

143

————. *The Westminster Confession and Modern Society.* Edinburgh, Scotland: Scottish Reformed Fellowship, 1972.

Le Roux. *Kultuur en Totaliteit* (Culture and Totality). Stellenbosch, South Africa: University of Stellenbosch, 1971.

Lippert. *The Evolution of Culture.* London, England: Geo. Allen & Unwin, 1931.

Masselink. *Common Grace and Christian Education.* Grand Rapids, Mich., 1954.

————. *General Revelation and Common Grace,* 1953.

Meeter. "Calvinism and Culture," in *The Basic Ideas of Calvinism.* Grand Rapids, Mich.: Kregel, 1967

Meland. *Faith and Culture.* New York, 1953.

Meyer. *Nog Nie Die Einde Nie* (Not Yet the End!). Cape Town, South Africa: Balkema, 1954.

Murray. "Common Grace," in *Westminster Theological Journal* V (November, 1942).

Niebuhr. *Christ and Culture.* New York: Harper Torchbook, 1956.

Philosophia Reformata (Reformed Philosophy). Netherlands (various issues).

Popma. "Cultuur" ("Culture"), in *Christelijke Encyclopaedie* (The Christian Encyclopaedia), 2nd ed., Kampen, Netherlands: J. H. Kok.

————. *Levensbeschouwing* (View of Life), vols. I-V. Amsterdam, Netherlands: Buijten & Schipperheijn, 1958.

Potgieter. "Die Teosentriese Universiteit" ("The God-centered University"), in *Gereformeerde Vaandel* (The Reformed Banner). Stellenbosch, South Africa.

————. *Die Verhouding Tussen Teologie en Filosofie by Calvyn* (The Relationship Between Theology and Philosophy in Calvin). Amsterdam, Netherlands: North Holland Publishing Co., 1939.

Potgieter & Stoker, eds. See Stoker & Potgieter, eds.

Puchinger. *Een Theologie in Discussie: over Prof. Dr. K. Schilder (Profeet, Dichter, Polemist) met als bijdrage het debat Schilder-*

Noordmans uit 1936. (A Theology in Discussion: on Prof. Dr. K. Schilder [Prophet, Poet, · Polemicist] with the debate between Schilder and Noordmans during 1936 as an appendix). Kampen, Netherlands: J. H. Kok, 1970.

Reid. "The Impact of Calvinism on Sixteenth Century Culture," in *International Reformed Bulletin* (October, 1967).

Richardson. *The Biblical Doctrine of Work.* London, England: SCM Press, 1963.

Ridderbos, H. N. "Eerherstel voor cultuur-theologie" ("Honorable Reinstallation of Cultural Theology"), in *Gereformeerd Weekblad* (Reformed Weekly). Kampen, Netherlands (1958).

Ridderbos, S. J. *De Theologische Cultuurbeschouwing van Abraham Kuyper* (The Theological View of Culture of Abraham Kuyper). Kampen, Netherlands: J. H. Kok, 1947.

————. *Rondom het Gemene Gratie Problem—over gemeene-gratie-beschouwingen van Schilder en De Graaf, . . . over Van Til en Barth* (Concerning the Problem of Common Grace—on the Common Grace Views of Schilder and De Graaf, . . . on Van Til and Barth). Kampen, Netherlands: J. H. Kok, 1949.

Rushdoony. *By What Standard?* Philadelphia: Presbyterian and Reformed Publishing Co., 1965.

————. *The Biblical Philosophy of History.* Nutley, N. J.: Presbyterian and Reformed Publishing Co., 1969.

————. *The Institutes of Biblical Law.* Nutley, N. J.: The Craig Press, 1973.

Schaeffer. *Art and the Bible.* Downers Grove, Ill.: Inter-Varsity Press, 1973.

———— *Genesis in Time and Space.* Downers Grove, Ill.: Inter-Varsity Press, 1972.

————. *The God Who Is There.* Downers Grove, Ill.: Inter-Varsity Press, 1968.

————. *The New Super Spirituality.* Downers Grove, Ill.: Inter-Varsity Press, 1972.

Schilder. *Christus en Cultuur* (Christ and Culture). Franeker, Netherlands: Wever, 1952.

————. *De Openbaring van Johannes en het Sociale Leven* (John's Revelation and Social Life). Delft, Netherlands: Meinema, n.d.

————. "Jezus Christus en het Cultuurleven" ("Jesus Christ and Cultural Life"), in *Jezus Christus en het Menschenleven* (Jesus Christ and Human Life). Culemborg, Netherlands: Uitgevers-bedrijf De Pauw, 1932.

————. "Vragen rond de Algemene Genade" ("Questions concerning General Grace"), in *Americana*, pp. 1-6 *College-verslagen der door Prof. Dr. Schilder in Amerika gehouden Lezingen, April 1939–June 1939* (Class Reports of Lectures held in America by Prof. Dr. Schilder, April 1939–June 1939), 1st ed. Kampen. Netherlands: cf. 1939 ed. Eerste Kamper Skryfkamer, Boven-meenstr. 74, 1939.

Seerveld. *A Christian Critique of Art.* Hamilton, Ontario, Canada: Guardian Publishing Co., 1963.

————. *A Christian Critique of. Literature.* Hamilton, Ontario, Canada: Guardian Publishing Co., 1964.

Snyman. *Calvinistiese Kultuurbeskouing* (Calvinistic View of Culture. Potchefstroom, South Africa: Institute for the Promotion of Calvinism, no. 5.

Stoker. "Arbeid—Wysgerig Benader" ("Labor—Considered Philosophically"), in *Bulletin van die Suid-Afrikaanse Vereniging vir die Bevordering van Christelike Wetenskap* (Bulletin of the South African Association for the Promotion of Christian Scholarship). Potchefstroom, South Africa (August, 1971).

————. *Die Wysbegeerte van die Skeppingsidee* (The Philosophy of the Idea of Creation). Pretoria, South Africa: De Bussy, 1933.

————. "Iets oor Kultuur en ons Kultuurstryd" ("Something About Culture and Our. Cultural Struggle"), in *Gereformeerde Vaandel* (The Reformed Banner) V, 7. Stellenbosch, South Africa.

————. *Kultuur en Roeping* (Culture and Vocation). Potchefstroom, South Africa: Potchefstroom University for Christian Higher Education, roneo.

————. *Mens en Tegniek Vandag* (Man and Technology Today). Pretoria, South Africa: Van Schaik, 1970.

Stoker & Potgieter, eds. *Koers in die Krisis* (Our Direction in the Crisis), vols. I-III. Stellenbosch, South Africa, 1936ff.

Thurneysen. "Christus und seine Zukunft" ("Christ and His Coming"), in *Zwischen den Zeiten* (Between the Times). Munich, Germany, 1931.

Tillich. *Theology of Culture*. New York: Oxford University Press, 1964.

Triton. *Whose World? The Christian's Attitude to the Material World, to Culture, Politics, Technology, Society*. London, England: Inter-Varsity Press, 1970.

Tydskrif vir Christelike Wetenskap (Journal for Christian Scholarship). Bloemfontein, South Africa (various issues).

Tylor. *Primitive Culture*. London, England, 1891.

Van Andel. *Ethiek van Arbeid en Rust* (Ethics of Work and Rest). Nijkerk, Netherlands: Callenbach, 1965.

―――. "The Christian and Culture," in *The Presbyterian Guardian* (January, 1944).

Van Baalen. *De Loochening der Gemeene Gratie—Gereformeerd of Doopersch?* (The Denial of Common Grace—Reformed or Anabaptistic?). Grand Rapids, Mich.: Eerdmans-Sevensma Co., 1922.

Van der Merwe. "Calvinisme en Kultuur" (Calvinism and Culture), in Stoker & Potgieter, eds., *Koers in die Krisis* (q.v.), I.

Van der Waal. *Het Cultuurmandaat in Discussie* (The Dominion Charter Under Discussion). Pretoria, South Africa: Servire, Villieria, 1971.

―――. "Ons politeuma" ("Our Citizenship"), in *Wat staat er eigenlijk?* (What Exactly Stands Written There?). Goes, Netherlands: Oosterbaan & Le Cointre, 1971.

―――. *Openbaring van Jezus Christus* (Revelation of Jesus Christ). Groningen, Netherlands: Uitgeverij De Vuurbaak, 1971, esp. pp. 107-132, 276-279.

―――. "Over de 'vreemd'ling hierbeneên' " ("On Strangers Here Below' "), in *Wat staat er Eigenlijk?* (as in "Ons Politeuma," above).

Van Dyk. *'n Kultuur-psigologiese Beskouing van die Wetenskap en die tegniek in die Krisis van die Westerse Wêreld* (A Cultural-Psychological View of Science and Technology in the Crisis of the

147

Western World). Potchefstroom, South Africa: Institute for the Promotion of Calvinism, no. 14.

Van Leeuwen. *Openbaring en Cultuur* (Revelation and Culture). Kampen, Netherlands: J. H. Kok, 1955.

Van Peursen. *Cultuur en Christelijk Geloof* (Culture and the Christian Faith). Kampen, Netherlands: J. H. Kok, 1955.

Van Riessen. *Mondigheid en de Machten* (Maturity and Power). Amsterdam, Netherlands: Buijten & Schipperheijn, 1967.

————. *Techniek en Cultuur* (Technology and Culture). Netherlands Royal Institute of Engineers, 1951, no. 17.

————. *The Society of the Future.* Philadelphia: Presbyterian and Reformed Publishing Co., 1952.

Van Ruler. *Kuypers Idee eener Christelijken Cultuur* (Kuyper's Idea of a Christian Culture). Netherlands: Nijkerk, n.d.

————. "Kuypers Leer van die Gemeene Gratie" ("Kuyper's Doctrine of Common Grace"), in *De Gereformeerde Kerk* (The Reformed Church). (October 7, 1937–December 15, 1938).

Van Til, C. *A Letter on Common Grace.* Phillipsburg, N. J.: Grotenhuis, n.d.

————. *Common Grace.* Philadelphia: Presbyterian and Reformed Publishing Co., 1954.

————. *Common Grace and Witness-Bearing.* Phillipsburg, N. J.: Grotenhuis, after 1955.

————. "Nature and Scripture," in *The Infallible Word.* Philadelphia: The Presbyterian Guardian Publishing Corporation, 1946.

————. *Particularism and Common Grace.* Phillipsburg, N. J.: Grotenhuis, after 1951.

Van Til, H. *The Calvinistic Concept of Culture.* Grand Rapids, Mich.: Baker, 1972.

Veenhof. *In Kuypers Lijn* (In Kuyper's Footsteps). Goes, Netherlands: Oosterbaan & Le Cointre, 1939.

Veldkamp. *Het Ambt der Gelovigen* (The Office of the Believers). Franeker, Netherlands: Wever, n.d.

Velema. "De genadeleer in de theologie van Kuyper" ("The Doctrine of Grace in Kuyper's Theology"), in *Kerk en Theologie* (Church and Theology). Wageningen, Netherlands, 1960.

―――. *De leer van de Heiligen Geest bij Abraham Kuyper* (Abraham Kuyper's Doctrine of the Holy Spirit). 's-Gravenhage, Netherlands, 1957.

Venter, E. A. *Die Gelowige in die Samelewing* (The Believer in Society). Bloemfontein, South Africa, n.d.

―――. "Calvyn en die Wetenskap" ("Calvin and Science"), in *Gereformeerde Vaandel* (Reformed Banner). Stellenbosch, South Africa.

Venter, C. N. *Kultuur en Versorgingswetenskap* (Culture and Welfare Science). Potchefstroom, South Africa: Potchefstroom University for Christian Higher Education, 1965.

―――. " 'n Calvinistiese Kultuurbeskouing, 1965" ("A Calvinistic View of Culture, 1965"), in *Die Atoomeeu 'in U lig'* (The Atomic Age 'in Thy light'). Potchefstroom, South Africa: Institute for the Promotion of Calvinism, 1965.

―――. " 'n Calvinistiese Kultuurbeskouing, 1969–1970"), ("A Calvinistic View of Culture, 1969–1970"), in *Koers* (Direction) XXXVII, nos. 3 & 4. Potchefstroom, South Africa.

―――. "Volkslewe en Kultuur" ("National Life and Culture"), in *Die Koninkryk van God* (The Kingdom of God). Potchefstroom, South Africa.

Venter, D. G. *Eindbestemming van die Skepping* (The Final Destination of Creation). Potchefstroom, South Africa: Die Evangelis, 1964.

Verbrugh. *Bouwen aan de Toekomst* (Building the Future). Dordrecht, Netherlands: Groen van Prinsterer Foundation, n.d.

Visscher. *De Schepping* (The Creation). Zwolle, Netherlands: La Riviere & Voorhoewe, 1930.

―――. *Het Paradijsprobleem* (The Paradise Problem). Zwolle, Netherlands, La Riviere & Voorhoewe, 1929.

Vriend. "Christ and Culture," in *Torch and Trumpet* I, 1 (1951).

Wallbank & Taylor. *Civilization Past and Present* (Chicago, Atlanta, Dallas, Palo Alto, Fair Lawn, N. J.: Scott, Foresman), 1960.

Wencelius. "Calvyn se Kunsfilosofie" ("Calvin's Philosophy of Art"), in Stoker & Potgieter, eds., *Koers in die Krisis* (q.v.), II.

―――――. *L'esthéthique de Calvin* (Calvin's Aesthetics). Strassbourg, France: Société d' Edition 'Les Belles Lettres.'

―――――. "The Word of God and Culture," in *The Word of God and the Reformed Faith*. Grand Rapids, Mich., 1942.

Wielenga. "Christendom en Cultuur" ("Christianity and Culture"), in *Het Wezen van het Christendom* (The Essence of Christianity). Kampen, Netherlands: J. H. Kok, n.d.

Wurth. "Bavinck en de Cultuur" ("Bavinck and Culture"), in *Bezinning* (Reflection) IX, no. 12 (December, 1954), Netherlands.

―――――. "Calvinistische Levensstijl" ("Calvinistic Life Style"), in Stoker and Potgieter, eds., *Koers in die Krisis* (q.v.), II.

―――――. "Christelijke Cultuurbeschouwing" ("Christian View of Culture"), in *Philosophia Reformata* (Reformed Philosophy). Kampen, Netherlands: J. H. Kok, 1st Quarter, 1938.

―――――. *Het Christelijk Leven* (The Christian Life). Kampen, Netherlands: J. H. Kok, 1948.

Zuidema. "Gemeene Gratie en Pro Rege bij Dr. Abr. Kuyper" ("Common Grace and 'For the King' in Dr. Abr. Kuyper"), in *Antirevolutionaire Staatkunde* (Anti-revolutionary Statecraft) XXIV, 1 (1954). Kampen, Netherlands.

LaVergne, TN USA
13 August 2010
193290LV00001B/1/A